Beyond ˊ

Frank Karsten and Karel Beckman

Beyond Democracy

Why democracy does not lead to solidarity, prosperity and liberty but to social conflict, runaway spending and a tyrannical government.

Beyond Democracy

Why democracy does not lead to solidarity, prosperity and liberty but to social conflict, runaway spending and a tyrannical government.

© 2012 Frank Karsten and Karel Beckman
www.beyonddemocracy.net

ISBN-13: 978-1467987691
ISBN-10: 1467987697

Cover Photo: Parthenon from South by Thermos

About the authors

Karel Beckman is a writer and journalist. He is chief editor of the online medium European Energy Review. Before that he worked as journalist at the Dutch financial newspaper Financieele Dagblad. His personal website is *www.charlieville.nl.*

Frank Karsten is founder of Stichting Meer Vrijheid (More Freedom Foundation), a Dutch libertarian organization which acts to reduce taxes and government intervention. He regularly appears in public to speak against the growing interference of the State in the lives of citizens. *www.meervrijheid.nl.*

Contents

Introduction
Democracy – the last taboo

"If there are any ills that democracy is suffering from today, they can only be cured by more democracy." This old quotation from an American politician shows in a nutshell how our democratic political system is generally viewed. People are prepared to agree that democracy may have its problems – they may even agree that many western parliamentary democracies, including the one in the US, may be on the brink of collapse – but they cannot conceive of an alternative. The only cure they can think of is, indeed, *more* democracy.

That our parliamentary democracy system is in crisis few would deny. Everywhere citizens in democratic countries are dissatisfied and deeply divided. Politicians complain that voters behave like spoiled children, citizens complain that politicians are deaf to their wishes. Voters have become notoriously fickle. They routinely switch their allegiance from one political party to another. They also feel increasingly attracted to radical and populist parties. Everywhere the political landscape is fragmenting, making it more and more difficult to overcome differences and form workable governments.

The existing political parties do not have an answer to these challenges. They are unable to develop real alternatives. They are trapped in rigid party structures, their ideals hijacked by special interest groups and lobbyists. Virtually no democratic government has been able to control its spending. Most democratic countries have been borrowing, spending and taxing so extensively that it resulted in a financial crisis that brought various countries to the brink of bankruptcy. And on the rare occasions when circumstances force governments to reduce their expenditures at least temporarily, the electorate rises up in protest at what they believe is an assault on their entitlements, making any kind of real cutbacks impossible.

Despite their spending sprees, almost all democratic countries suffer from permanently high unemployment rates. Large groups of people remain on the sidelines. Virtually no democratic country has made adequate provisions for their aging populations.

Typically all democratic societies suffer from an excess of bureaucracy and regulatory zeal. The tentacles of the State reach into everyone's lives. There are rules and regulations for everything under the sun. And every problem is addressed through more rules and regulations rather than genuine solutions.

At the same time democratic governments do a bad job carrying out what many people would consider their most important task –

> *It is no exaggeration to say that democracy has become a religion – a modern, secular religion.*

maintaining law and order. Crime and vandalism are rampant. Police and the justice system are unreliable, incompetent and often downright corrupt. Harmless behavior is criminalized. As a percentage of its population, the US has the largest number of people in prison in the world. Many of these people are in jail for perfectly innocuous behavior, simply because their habits are considered offensive by the majority.

People's confidence in their democratically elected politicians has reached all-time lows according to various studies. There is a deep-rooted distrust of governments, political rulers, elites and international agencies who seem to have put themselves above the law. Many people have become pessimistic about the future. They fear that their children will be worse off than they are. They fear the invasion of immigrants, are worried that their own culture is under threat and long for times gone by.

The democratic faith

Although the crisis of democracy is widely acknowledged, there is virtually no criticism of the democratic system itself. There is virtually no one who blames democracy as such for the problems we are experiencing. Invariably political leaders – whether left, right or in-between – promise to tackle our problems with more democracy, not less. They promise they will listen to the people and put the public interest above private interests. They promise they will cut down on bureaucracy, become more transparent, deliver better services – make the system work again. But they never call the desirability of the democratic system itself into question. They'd much sooner argue that our problems are caused by too much freedom than too much democracy. The only difference between progressives and conservatives is that the former are likely to complain about too much economic freedom, and the latter about too much social freedom. This at a time when there have never been so many laws and taxes have never been so high!

In fact, criticism of the democratic idea is more or less taboo in western societies. You are allowed to criticize how democracy is being put into practice, or to castigate the current political leaders or parties – but criticizing the democratic ideal as such is 'not done'.

It is no exaggeration to say that democracy has become a religion – a modern, secular religion. You could call it the largest faith on earth. All but eleven countries – Myanmar, Swaziland, the Vatican and some Arab nations – claim to be democracies, even if only in name. This belief in the God of democracy is closely linked to the worship of the national democratic state that arose in the course of the 19th century. God and the Church were replaced with the State as society's Holy Father. Democratic elections are the ritual by which we pray to the State for employment, shelter, health, security, education. We have absolute faith in this Democratic State. We believe He can take care of everything. He is the rewarder, the judge, the all-knowing, the almighty. We even expect Him to solve all our personal and social problems.

The beauty of the Democratic God is that He provides His good works completely selflessly. As God, the State has no self-interest. He is the pure guardian of the public interest. He also doesn't cost anything. He freely deals out bread, fish and other favors.

At least, that's how it seems to people. Most people tend to see only the benefits the government delivers, not the costs. One reason for this is that the government collects taxes in many roundabout and indirect ways – by requiring businesses to collect sales taxes for example, or by requiring employers to collect social security taxes, or by borrowing money in the financial markets (which will someday have to be paid back by taxpayers) or by inflating the money supply – so that people don't realize how much of their income is actually confiscated by the government. Another reason is that the results of government actions are visible and tangible, but all the things that could and would have been done if the government had not confiscated people's money in the first place, remain invisible. The war planes that get built are there for all to see, all the things that don't get done because the public's money was spent on war planes, remain invisible.

The democratic faith has become so deeply ingrained that democracy for most people is synonymous with everything that is (politically) right and moral. Democracy means freedom (everyone is allowed to vote), equality (each vote counts equally), fairness (everyone is equal), unity (we all decide together), peace (democracies never start unjust wars). In this way of thinking the only alternative to democracy is dictatorship. And dictatorship, of course, represents everything that is bad: lack of freedom, inequality, war, injustice.

In his famous 1989 essay 'The End of History?', the neo-conservative thinker Francis Fukuyama went as far as to declare that the modern western democratic system is the climax of mankind's political evolution. Or, as he put it, today we are witnessing 'the universalization of Western liberal democracy as *the final form of human government'*. Obviously only very evil minds (terrorists, fundamentalists, fascists) would dare speak out against such a sacred notion.

Democracy = collectivism

Yet this is precisely what we will do in this book: speak out against the God of democracy, especially national parliamentary democracy. The democratic decision-making model is useful in some contexts, in small communities or within associations. But a national parliamentary democracy, which almost all western countries have, has far more drawbacks than advantages. Parliamentary democracy, we argue, is unjust, leads to bureaucracy and stagnation, undermines freedom, independence and enterprise, and inevitably leads to antagonism, meddling, lethargy and overspending. And not because certain politicians fail in their job – or because the wrong party is in charge – but because that's how the system works.

The hallmark of democracy is that 'the people' decide how society should be organized. In other words, all of us 'together' decide on everything that concerns us. How high taxes should be, how much money needs to be spent on child care and on the elderly, at what age people are allowed to drink alcoholic beverages, how much employers must pay for the pensions of their employees, what should be put on a product label, what children must learn at school, how much money should be spent on development aid or on renewable energy or on sports education or on orchestras, how a bar owner should run his bar and whether his guests are allowed to smoke, how a house should be built, how high interest rates should be, how much money needs to circulate in the economy, whether banks should be rescued with taxpayers' money if they threaten to go bankrupt, who is allowed to call himself a physician, who is allowed to start a hospital, whether people are allowed to die when they are tired of life, and if and when the nation is at war. In a democracy, 'the people' are expected to decide on all these matters - and thousands of others.

Thus, democracy is by definition a *collectivist* system. It's socialism through the backdoor. The basic idea behind it is that it is desirable and right that all important decisions about the physical, social and economic organization of society are taken by the collective, the people. And the people authorize their representatives in parliament – in other words, the State – to take these decisions for them. In other words, in a democracy the whole fabric of society is geared towards the State.

Clearly then it is misleading to claim that democracy is, somehow, the inevitable climax of the political evolution of mankind. That's just propaganda to disguise that democracy represents a very specific political orientation. For which there are indeed plenty of reasonable alternatives.

One of those alternatives is called: freedom. Or liberalism – in the classical sense of the word (which has an entirely different meaning from liberalism as the word is used today

> That freedom is not the same as democracy is not hard to see. Consider this: do we decide democratically how much money everyone should spend on clothes?

in the US). That freedom is not the same as democracy is not hard to see. Consider this: do we decide democratically how much money everyone should spend on clothes? Or what supermarket we go to? Clearly not. Everyone decides that for themselves. And this freedom of choice works fine. So why does it work better if all other things that affect us – from our workplace, health care and pensions to our pubs and clubs – are decided upon democratically?

In fact, couldn't it be the case that this very fact – that we decide on everything democratically, that virtually all economic and social issues are controlled by or through the State – is the underlying cause of the many things that are wrong in our society? That bureaucracy, government meddling, parasitism, crime, corruption, unemployment, inflation, low educational standards, et cetera, are not due to a *lack* of democracy, but rather are *caused* by democracy? That they go with democracy like empty shops and Trabant cars went with communism?

That is what we hope to show you in this book.

This book is divided into three parts. In the first part we discuss our faith in the God of parliamentary democracy. Like any religion, democracy has a set of beliefs – dogmas that everyone accepts as indisputable truths. We present these in the form of 13 popular myths about democracy.

In the second part we describe the practical consequences of the democratic system. We try to show why democracy inevitably leads to stagnation and what makes it inefficient and unjust.

In the third section we outline an alternative to democracy, namely a political system based on self-determination of the individual, which is characterized by decentralization, local governance and diversity.

Despite our criticism of the current national-democratic system, we are optimistic about the future. One reason why many people are pessimistic is that they feel that the current system is going nowhere, but they can't imagine an attractive alternative. They know that government to a large extent controls their lives but they can't control government. The only alternatives they can imagine are forms of dictatorship, such as the 'Chinese model' or some form of nationalism or fundamentalism.

But that's where they are mistaken. Democracy does not mean freedom. It is just as much a form of dictatorship – the dictatorship of the majority and the State. Nor is it synonymous with justice, equality, solidarity, or peace.

Democracy is a system that was introduced about 150 years ago in most western countries, for various reasons, for one thing to achieve socialist ideas within liberal societies. Whatever the reasons at the time, there are no good reasons now to retain the national parliamentary democracy. It doesn't work anymore. It is time for a new political ideal, in which productivity and solidarity are not organized on the basis of democratic dictatorship, but are the result of voluntary relationships between people. We hope to convince our readers that the possibility of realizing such an ideal is greater than many people today may imagine - and worth the effort of pursuing.

I. Myths of democracy

Myth 1
Every vote counts

We always hear this during election time. The claim that your vote really counts. Which is true – for one in a hundred million (if we are talking about US presidential elections). But if you have a one in a 100 million influence on the outcome of a process, or 0.000001%, in practice that's zero influence. The chance that your vote decides who will win the election is astronomically small.

And it's actually even worse, because the vote you cast is not for a specific policy or decision. It's a vote for a candidate or political party that will take decisions *on your behalf.* But you have no influence whatsoever on the decisions that person or party takes! You cannot control them. For four years they can decide what they want, and there is nothing you can do about it. You can bombard them with e-mails, fall down on your knees in front of them or curse them – but they decide.

Every year the government takes many thousands of decisions. This one vote of yours, for someone who can do whatever they like without further consultation with you, has no measurable impact on any of those decisions.

> *Voting is the illusion of influence in exchange for the loss of freedom.*

The vote you cast is usually not even a real choice. It is more an indication of a vague preference. There rarely is a person or political party with which you agree in all respects. Suppose you don't want money being spent on Third World aid, or the war in Afghanistan. You can then vote for a party that opposes it. But perhaps that party is also in favor of raising the retirement age, something you happen to disagree with.

What is more, after a party or person which you may have voted for, has been elected, they all too often break their election promises. Then what can you do? You should be able to sue them for fraud, but you can't. At best you can vote for a different party or candidate after four years – with just as little result.

Voting is the illusion of influence in exchange for the loss of freedom. When Tom or Jane show up at the ballot box, they think they are influencing the direction in which the country is going. And to a very small extent that is true. At the same time 99.9999% of the voters decide on the direction in which Tom's and Jane's lives are going. In this way they lose much more control over their own lives than they gain in influence over the lives of others. They would have much more 'influence' if they could just make their own choices. For example, if they could decide for themselves what they spend their money on, without first having to pay half of their income to the government through various taxes.

Or to give another example, in our democratic system, people have little direct control over the education of their children. If they want to change educational practices and want to have more influence than just through the ballot box, they must join or start a lobby group, or present politicians with petitions, or organize protests at government buildings. There are organizations of parents that try to influence educational policy in this way. It takes lots of time and energy and has virtually no effect. It would be infinitely simpler and more efficient if the State would not interfere with education, and teachers, parents and students could make their own choices, both individually and together.

Of course the ruling class continually urges people to vote. They always emphasize that by voting people really do have influence over government policies. But what actually matters to them is that a high turnout gives them a stamp of approval, a moral right to rule over people.

Many people believe it is a moral duty to participate in elections. It is often said that if you don't vote, you have no right to have your say in public debates or to complain about political decisions. After all, you didn't cast your ballot, so your opinion doesn't count anymore. People who claim this apparently can't imagine that there are some people who refuse to subscribe to the illusion of influence that democracy sells. They suffer from the Stockholm syndrome. They have come to love their captors and don't realize that they are trading in their autonomy for the power that politicians and administrators hold over them.

Myth 2
The people rule in a democracy

This is the basic idea of democracy. It's what democracy literally means, government by the people. But do the people really govern in a democracy?

The first problem is that 'the people' do not exist. There are only millions of individuals with as many opinions and interests. How can they govern together? That's impossible. Like a Dutch comedian once said: "Democracy is the will of the people. Every morning I am surprised to read in the newspaper what I want."

Let's face it, nobody will say something like "the consumer wants Microsoft" or 'the people want Pepsi". Some do and some don't. The same applies to political preferences.

In addition, it is not really 'the people' who decide in a democracy, but 'the majority' of the people, or rather, the majority of voters. The minority apparently doesn't belong to 'the people'. That seems a little strange. Is not everyone part of the people? As a customer of Wal-Mart, you don't want groceries from another supermarket forced down your throat, but that's how things work in a democracy. If you happen to belong to the losing side in the elections, you must dance to the tune of the winners.

But okay, let's assume that the majority is the same as the people. Is it really true then that the people decide? Let's see. There are two types of democracies: direct and indirect (or representative). In a direct democracy, everyone votes on every decision that is made, as in a referendum. In an indirect democracy people vote for other people who then take decisions for them. Clearly in the second case people have much less to say than in the first. However, almost all modern democracies are indirect, although they may throw in occasional referenda.

To justify the representational system it is argued that a) it would be impractical to hold referenda on all the many decisions that the government has to take every day and b) people do not have enough expertise to decide on all kinds of complex issues.

Argument a) may have been plausible in the past, because it was difficult to provide everyone with the necessary information and let them have their say, except in very small communities. Today, this argument is no longer valid. With the Internet and other modern communication technologies, it's easy to let large groups participate in decision-making processes and hold referenda. Yet this almost never happens. Why not have a referendum on whether the US should go to war in Afghanistan or Libya or wherever? After all, the people rule, don't they? Why can't they take these decisions then that are so crucial to their lives? In fact of course, everyone knows that there are many decisions being taken that the majority would not support if they were brought to a vote. The idea that 'the people govern' is simply a myth.

But what about argument b)? Aren't most issues too complex to be brought to a vote? Hardly. Whether a mosque should be built somewhere, what should be the legal drinking age, how high minimum sentences should be for certain crimes, whether more or fewer highways need to be built, how high the national debt should be, whether or not some foreign country should be invaded, and so on – these are all pretty clear propositions. If our rulers take democracy seriously, shouldn't they at least let people vote directly on a number of them?

Or does argument b) mean that people are not intelligent enough to be able to form reasonable opinions on all sorts of social and economic issues? If that is so, how can they be smart enough to understand the various election programs and vote on the basis of them? Anyone who advocates democracy must at least assume that people know a thing or two and are able to understand plain language. Besides, why would the politicians that are voted into office necessarily be smarter than the voters who elect them? Do politicians mysteriously have access to the fountain of wisdom and knowledge while voters don't? Or do they have higher moral values than the average citizen? There is no evidence for that whatsoever.

Defenders of democracy will perhaps argue that, even if people are not stupid, no person has sufficient knowledge and intelligence to take decisions on the complex issues that deeply affect

> *It is not 'the will of the people', but the will of politicians – prompted by groups of professional lobbyists, interest groups and activists – that reigns in a democracy.*

the lives of millions of individuals. That is undoubtedly true, but the same goes for the politicians and civil servants who take those decisions in a democracy. For example, how can they know what kind of education parents, teachers and students want? Or what is the best education? People all have their own desires and their own views on what good education is. And most of them are intelligent enough to at least decide what is good for themselves and their children. But this flies in the face of the centralized one-size-fits-all approach of democracy.

It seems, then, that in our democracy the people don't rule at all. Nor is this really such a surprise. Everyone knows that governments regularly take decisions that most people oppose. It is not 'the will of the people', but the will of politicians – prompted by groups of professional lobbyists, interest groups and activists – that reigns in a democracy. Big Oil, Big Agra, Big Pharma, Big Medicine, the Military-industrial complex, Wall Street – they all know how to work the system to their advantage. A small elite takes the decisions – often behind the scenes. Not bothered by what 'the people' want, they squander our savings on war and aid programs, allow mass-immigration few citizens want, build up enormous deficits, spy on their citizens, start wars few voters want, spend our money on subsidies for special interest groups, enter into agreements – like the monetary union in the EU or NAFTA – that benefit the unproductive at the expense of the productive. Did we all want this democratically or was it what the rulers wanted?

How many people would actually voluntarily transfer thousands of dollars to the government's bank account so that soldiers can fight in Afghanistan in their name? Why don't we ask the people just for once? Don't they rule?

It's often said that democracy is a good way to limit the power of the rulers, but as we can see this turns out to be just another myth. The rulers can do pretty much what they want!

Moreover, the power of politicians extends much further than their actions in parliament and government. When they are driven out of office by the voters, they often land lucrative jobs in the countless organizations that exist in a close symbiosis with the State – broadcasting companies, labor unions, housing associations, universities, NGO's, lobbying groups, think tanks, and the thousands of advisory firms that live off the State like molds on a rotten tree trunk. In other words, a change of government does not necessarily mean a change in who is holding power in society. Democratic accountability is much more limited than it seems.

It is also noteworthy that it is far from easy to participate in elections in the United States. To be allowed to run in federal elections, you have to comply with legislation covering 500 pages. The rules are so complex that they cannot be understood by laypersons.

Yet, despite all this, the advocates of democracy always insist that 'we voted for it' when government implements some new law. This implies that 'we' no longer have the right to oppose such a measure. But this argument is rarely used consistently. Gays will use it to defend gay rights, but do not accept it when a democratic country prohibits homosexuality. Environmental activists demand that democratically decided environmental measures are enforced, but feel free to perform illegal protests if they disagree with other democratic decisions. In those cases apparently 'we' did not vote for it.

Myth 3
The majority is right

But let's assume for a moment, for the sake of argument, that the people really govern in a democracy and that every vote really counts. Will the outcome of this process automatically be right or good? After all, that's why we have a democracy, don't we – so that we do the right thing? But it's hard to see why or how the democratic process would necessarily lead to good or right results. If many people believe in something, that doesn't make it true. There are lots of examples in the past of collective delusions. For example, people used to think that animals could not experience pain or that the earth was flat, or that the king or emperor was the representative of God on earth.

Nor is something morally right or fair just because many people are in favor of it. Think of all the collective crimes that have been committed by people in the past. Abominations like slavery or the persecution of Jews were once considered perfectly acceptable by most people.

Let's face it: people are usually guided by self-interest in the way they vote. They vote for parties that they expect will benefit them the most. They know that the costs that come with the benefits they receive are

> *In a democracy, moral considerations are trumped by the will of the majority. Quantity trumps quality – the number of people that wants something overrides considerations of morality and rationality.*

borne by all people. Is this fair or desirable? The embarrassing truth is that people are most likely to be in favor of democracy because they hope or expect to belong to the majority, so they can benefit from plundering the wealth of the rest. They hope that their burdens will be shared by others and their benefits paid for by others. That's rather the opposite of moral behavior.

Are we exaggerating? If you and your friends rob someone on the street, you will get punished. If the majority passes a law to rob the minority (a new tax on alcohol or cigarettes for example), it is a democratic decision and it is thereby legal. But what is the difference with the street robbery?

When you think about it, you have to conclude that the basic mechanism of democracy – the fact that the majority calls the shots – is fundamentally immoral. In a democracy, moral considerations are trumped by the will of the majority. Quantity trumps quality – the number of people that wants something overrides considerations of morality and rationality.

The 19th Century British politician and writer Auberon Herbert had this to say about the logic and morality of democracy:

> "Five men are in a room. Because three men take one view and two another, have the three men any moral right to enforce their view on the other two men? What magical power comes over the three men that because they are one more in number than the two men, therefore they suddenly become possessors of the minds and bodies of these others? As long as they were two to two, so long we may suppose each man remained master of his own mind and body; but from the moment that another man, acting Heaven only knows from what motives, has joined himself to one party or the other, that party has become straightway possessed of the souls and bodies of the other party. Was there ever such a degrading and indefensible superstition? Is it not the true lineal descendant of the old superstitions about emperors and high priests and their authority over the souls and bodies of men?"

Myth 4
Democracy is politically neutral

Democracy is compatible with any political direction. After all, the voters determine the political preferences of the party or parties in charge. Thus, the system itself transcends all differences in political outlook: it is, in itself, neither left nor right, socialist nor capitalist, conservative nor progressive.

That's how it seems anyway. Yet this is at best a half truth. In reality democracy does embody a specific political direction.

Democracy is by definition a *collectivist* idea, namely the idea that we have to decide everything together and all must then abide by those decisions. This means that in a democracy pretty much everything is a public matter. *There are no fundamental limits to this collectivization.* If the majority (or rather, the government) want it, they can decide that we all have to wear a harness when walking the streets because it is safer. Or dress up like clowns because it would make people laugh. No individual liberty is sacred. This leaves the door open to ever increasing government interference. And ever increasing meddling is exactly what happens in democratic societies.

True, political trends may fluctuate and often backlashes occur – for example, from more to less regulation and back again – but in the long run western democracies have steadily advanced in the direction of more government interference, greater dependence on the State and higher public spending.

This was perhaps not so visible in the days of the Cold War, when Western democracies were compared to totalitarian states like the Soviet Union and Mao's China, which made them look relatively free. In those days it was less noticeable that we ourselves were also becoming more and more collectivist. Since the 1990s, however, after communism collapsed, it became clear that our welfare states had gone a long way in the same direction. Now we are being overtaken by newly emerging economies that offer more freedom, lower taxes, and less regulation than our own systems.

Of course many democratic politicians say they are for "the free market". Their actions show otherwise. Consider the Republican Party, which is often considered the party of free enterprise. They have come to embrace virtually all the major interventionist policies advanced by their leftist rivals – the welfare state, high taxes, high government spending, public housing, labor laws, minimum wages, foreign interventions – and added some of their own, such as subsidies for banks and big business, and laws against victimless crimes such as drug use and prostitution. Despite occasional reversions and bouts of "deregulation", under both Parties the power of the State has steadily grown, no matter how much the Republicans claim they are in favor of free enterprise. It is a fact that under the Republican 'conservative' President Ronald Reagan government spending went up, not down. Under the Republican administration of George W. Bush government spending did not go up – it skyrocketed. This shows that democracy is not neutral, but inherently tends towards an increase of collectivism and government power, whoever is in power at any one moment.

Government Spending, % of GDP										
	1870	1913	1920	1937	1960	1980	1990	2000	2005	2009
Austria	10.5	17	14.7	20.6	35.7	48.1	38.6	52.1	50.2	52.3
Belgium	8	13.8	22.1	21.8	30.3	58.6	54.8	49.1	52	54
Britain	9.4	12.7	26.2	30	32.2	43	39.9	36.6	40.6	47.2
Canada			16.7	25	28.6	38.8	46	40.6	39.2	43.8
France	12.6	17	27.6	29	34.6	46.1	49.8	51.6	53.4	56
Germany	10	14.8	25	34.1	32.4	47.9	45.1	45.1	46.8	47.6
Italy	13.7	17.1	30.1	31.1	30.1	42.1	53.4	46.2	48.2	51.9
Japan	8.8	8.3	14.8	25.4	17.5	32	31.3	37.3	34.2	39.7
Netherlands	9.1	9	13.5	19	33.7	55.8	54.1	44.2	44.8	50
Spain		11	8.3	13.2	18.8	32.2	42	39.1	38.4	45.8
Sweden	5.7	10.4	10.9	16.5	31	60.1	59.1	52.7	51.8	52.7
Switzerland	16.5	14	17	24.1	17.2	32.8	33.5	33.7	37.3	36.7
U.S.A.	7.3	7.5	12.1	19.7	27	31.4	33.3	32.8	36.1	42.2
Average	10.4	12.7	18.4	23.8	28.4	43.8	44.7	43.2	44.1	47.7

(Source: Economist, March 17th 2011)

This general trend is reflected in the steady growth of public spending. At the beginning of the 20th century public expenditure as a percentage of gross national product was typically around 10 percent in most western democracies. Now it's around 50 percent. So for six months of the year, people have become serfs working for the State.

In more free – and less democratic – times the tax burden was much lower than today. For centuries England had a system in which the king had the right to spend money, but not to raise taxes, and Parliament had the right to tax, but not to spend money.

Consequently, domestic taxes were relatively low. In the 20th century, when Britain became more democratic, taxes went up steeply.

The American Revolution started as a tax revolt by American colonists against the mother country Great Britain. The founders of the United States liked democracy just as much as they liked high taxes, which is to say, not at all. The word 'democracy' does not occur anywhere in the Declaration of Independence or in the Constitution.

In the 19th century, the tax burden in the United States was a few percent at most, except in times of war. Income tax didn't exist and was even forbidden by the Constitution. But as the United States were transformed from a decentralized, federal state into a national parliamentary democracy, government power steadily increased. Thus, for example, in 1913 the income tax was introduced and the Federal Reserve System was set up.

Another telling example can be seen in the Code of Federal Regulations (CFR)– which lists all laws enacted by the federal government. In 1925 this was just a single book. In 2010 it had mushroomed into more than 200 volumes, of which the index alone takes up more than 700 pages. It contains rules for everything under the sun – from how a watchband should look to how onion rings should be prepared in restaurants. Just during the presidency of George W. Bush, 1000 pages of federal regulations were added each year, reports The Economist. According to the same magazine, from 2001 to 2010 America's tax code grew from 1.4 million words to 3.8 million words.

Many proposed bills in Congress are so bloated that Congressmen don't even bother to read them before voting on them. In short, the advent of democracy has led to greatly expanded government interference in the United States, even though people often claim that America is a 'free' country.

In other western democracies a similar development has taken place. For example, in the Netherlands, where the authors of this book happen to come from, the total tax burden was 14 percent of Gross Domestic Product in 1850. Now it's 55 percent, according to a study from the Dutch Central Planning Bureau. According to another study, government spending as a percentage of national income was 10 percent in 1900 and 52 percent in 2002.

The number of laws and regulations in the Netherlands has also grown steadily. The number of laws on the books increased by 72 percent between 1980 and 2004, according to a study by the Scientific Research and Documentation Center of the Dutch Department of Justice. In 2004 the Netherlands had a total of 12,000 laws and regulations on the books, containing over 140,000 articles.

One problem with all these laws is that they tend to reinforce each other. In other words, one rule leads to another. For example, if you have a system of state-imposed health care insurance, the government is induced to try to force people to adopt (supposedly) healthy lifestyles. After all, it is said, 'we' all pay for the high medical costs of people who live unhealthily. This is true, but only because the government put in place a collectivized system to begin with. This type of health fascism is typical for democratic countries and is routinely accepted nowadays by most people. They find it perfectly normal that the government decrees that they should not eat fatty foods or sugar, that they should not smoke, that they should wear helmets or seatbelts, and so on. These are all straightforward violations of individual freedom of course.

One could argue that in recent decades freedom has advanced in a number of sectors. In many western countries private ('commercial') television companies have broken the monopolies of national broadcasting stations, opening hours of shops have expanded, air traffic was deregulated, the telecoms market was liberalized, and in many countries conscription was abolished. However, many of these achievements had to be wrested from the hands of democratic politicians. In many cases, these changes could not be stopped by politicians, as they were the result of technological developments (such as in the media or in telecoms) or of competition from other countries (as in the case of airline deregulation). These developments may be compared to the collapse of communism in the former Soviet Union. That did not happen because those in power wanted to give up their power, but because they had no choice – because the system was broken and could not be fixed. In the same way our democratic politicians regularly have to surrender bits of their power.

But our politicians usually manage to recover their lost ground fairly quickly. Thus, the freedom on the internet is more and more being restrained by government interference.

> *Actually, in its essence, democracy is a totalitarian ideology, though not as extreme as Nazism, fascism or communism.*

Freedom of speech is eroded by anti-discrimination laws. Intellectual property rights (patents and copyrights) are used to reign in the freedom of producers and consumers. The liberalization of markets is usually accompanied by the establishment of new bureaucracies intended to regulate the new markets. These bureaucratic agencies then tend to become ever larger and introduce ever more rules. In the Netherlands, sectors such as energy and telecoms were indeed liberalized, but at the same time new regulatory agencies were established – six of them in the last ten years.

In the US, according to researchers from the University of Virginia, the cost of federal regulations rose 3% from 2003 to 2008 to $1.75 trillion a year, or 12% of GDP. After 2008, waves of new regulations were introduced in the financial markets, the oil industry, the food industry and doubtless many other business sectors. In Europe businesses and households not only have their national governments to cope with, they also have to suffer an additional layer of regulations coming out of the European Union in Brussels. And whereas in the 1990s, liberalization was all the rage in Brussels, the trend nowadays is the reverse: towards ever more (re-)regulation.

In short, in practice democracy is not politically neutral. The system is collectivist in nature and leads to more and more government intervention and less and less individual freedom. This is so because people keep on making demands from government and want others to pay the costs.

Actually, in its essence, democracy is a totalitarian ideology, though not as extreme as Nazism, fascism or communism. In principle, no freedom is sacred in a democracy, every aspect of the individual's life is potentially subject to government control. At the end of the day, the minority is completely at the mercy of the whims of the majority. Even if a democracy has a constitution limiting the powers of the government, this constitution too can be amended by the majority. The only fundamental right you have in a democracy, besides running for office, is the right to vote for a political party. With that solitary vote you hand over your independence and your freedom to the will of the majority.

Real freedom is the right to choose *not* to participate in the system and *not* to have to pay for it. As a consumer, you aren't free if you are forced to choose between different TV sets, no matter how many brands you can choose from. You're only free if you can decide *not* to buy a TV set. In a democracy you have to buy what the majority has chosen – like it or not.

Myth 5
Democracy leads to prosperity

Many democratic countries are wealthy and therefore people often think that democracy is necessary to achieve prosperity. Actually, the reverse is true. Democracy doesn't lead to prosperity, it *destroys* wealth.

It's true that many *western* democracies are prosperous. Elsewhere in the world you don't see that correlation. Singapore, Hong Kong and a number of Gulf states are not democratic, though prosperous. Many countries in Africa and Latin America are democratic, but not wealthy, except for a small elite. Western countries are not prosperous because of democracy but rather despite of it. Their prosperity is due to the tradition of liberty that characterizes these countries, as a result of which the State is not yet in complete control over their economies. But this tradition is steadily weakened by democracy. The private sector is steadily being eroded, a process that threatens to destroy the fabulous wealth that was built up in the west over centuries.

Prosperity is created wherever the rights of individuals are adequately protected – in particular property rights. To put it differently, wealth is created *wherever people are able to own the fruits of their labor.* In that situation people are motivated to work hard, take risks and use the available resources efficiently.

On the other hand, if people are forced to cede the fruits of their labor to the State – which is partly the case in a democracy – they are less motivated to do their best.

> *In a democracy citizens are encouraged to gain advantages at the expense of others – or to pass on their burdens to others.*

Moreover, the State will inevitably use these resources inefficiently. After all, the (democratic) rulers didn't have to work to obtain the resources – and have very different objectives from the people who produced them.

How does this work in a democracy? You can compare it to a group of ten people who have dinner in a restaurant and decide in advance to split the bill evenly. Since 90 percent of the bill will be paid by the others, everyone is motivated to order expensive dishes, which they would not have done if they had had to pay the bill themselves. Conversely, since any individual saving benefits any person for only 10 percent, no one has an incentive to be frugal. The result is that the total bill ends up being much higher than if everyone had paid for themselves.

In economics, this phenomenon is known as 'the tragedy of the commons'. A common is a collectively owned piece of land used by several farmers. The farmers who share a common have a natural incentive to let their cows graze as much as possible (at the expense of others), and no incentive to removing their cows on time (because then the pasture would be grazed barren by the cattle of the other farmers). So, since the meadow is owned by all and therefore by nobody, the result is overgrazing.

Democracy works the same way. Citizens are encouraged to gain advantages at the expense of others – or to pass on their burdens to others. People vote for political parties that let others pay for their personal wishes (free education, higher welfare benefits, subsidies for child care, more freeways, and so on). In the example of the dinner, things might not get out of hand too much, because in a small group, people are restrained by social control, but with millions of voters in a democracy that doesn't work.

Politicians are elected to manipulate this system. They manage the 'public' goods. They don't own those, so they don't have to be economical. On the contrary, they have an incentive to spend as much as possible, so that they can get the credits and let their successors pay the bills. After all, they need to please the voters. That is more important to them than the long-term interest of the country. The result is inefficiency and wastefulness.

Not only are politicians strongly tempted to overspend, they also have an incentive to take as much for themselves as they can while they are in charge of 'public funds'. After all, once they are out of office, they cannot so easily enrich themselves anymore.

This system is disastrous for the economy. Exactly how disastrous, people have yet to realize fully. The bill for the spending sprees our democratic governments have indulged in for the most part still has to be paid.

The huge government debts are the result of the huge budget deficits which – not coincidentally – virtually all democratic countries suffer from. In the United States the democratic dinner has gotten so out of control that the national debt now stands at over $14,000 billion; roughly $50,000 per capita. In most European countries the situation is the same. The Dutch national debt rose to €380 billion at the end of 2010 or almost € 25,000 per capita. These debts will have to be repaid sometime, by the taxpayer. A lot of money is coughed up by the taxpayer already merely to pay the interest on the debt. In the Netherlands the interest on the national debt amounted to about € 22 billion in 2009, more than was spent on defense and infrastructure. This is all a pure waste of money, the result of past squandering of taxpayers' money.

But the rot goes even deeper. Our democratic politicians not only collect taxes that they subsequently waste, they have also managed to secure control over our financial system – our money. Through central banks like the Federal Reserve and the European Central Bank our democratic governments determine what constitutes money ('legal tender'), how much money is created and gets injected into the economy and how high interest rates are. At the same time they have severed the link, which used to exist, between paper money and underlying values, such as gold. *Our entire financial system – including all our savings and retirement funds, all the money we think we possess – is based on fiat paper money issued by the State.*

The advantage of this system to our governments is evident. They have a 'money tap' they can turn on whenever they want to. No absolute monarch in the past has ever had anything like it! Democratic leaders can just 'pump up' the economy (and fill up their own coffers) if they want to boost their popularity. They do this through the Central Bank, which in turn uses private banks to carry out the process of issuing the money. The system is designed in such a way that private banks are granted special permission to lend out a multiple of the money their clients deposit (fractional reserve banking). Thus, through various tricks ever more paper or electronic money is injected into the economy.

This has several negative consequences. To begin with, the value of money decreases. That process has already been going on for a century. The dollar has lost 95 percent of its value since the Federal Reserve system was created in 1913. That's why we as citizens notice products and services getting steadily more expensive. In a truly free market prices have a tendency to continually drop as a result of productivity improvements and competition. But in our government-manipulated system, in which the money supply is constantly increased, prices go up all the time. Some people benefit from this (e.g. those who have large debts, like the government itself), others are worse off, like people who live on a fixed pension or have savings.

The second consequence is that with all the new money pumping up the economy, one artificial boom after another is fueled. Hence we had a real estate boom, a commodities boom, a stock market boom. But all these miracles are based on hot air – all the booms turn out to be bubbles that are popped sooner or later. They happened only because the markets were flooded by easy credit and all the players could load themselves with debts. But such parties cannot continue forever. When it becomes clear that the debts can't be repaid, the bubbles explode. That's how recessions come into being.

The authorities usually respond to recessions as you would expect from democratic politicians, namely by creating yet more artificial money and pumping ever larger amounts of it into the economy (while of course blaming 'free markets' or 'speculators' for the crisis). They do this because voters expect it from them. The voters want the party to continue as long as possible – and the politicians usually fulfill their wishes because they want to be reelected. The American writer and politician Benjamin Franklin saw the problem as early as the 18th century. "When the people find that they can vote themselves money, that will herald the end of the republic," he wrote.

Turning on the printing press usually provides some solace – but it's always temporary. Right now we seem to have reached the point where no new bubbles can be created without wrecking the system altogether. The authorities don't know what to do anymore. If they continue to create money, they run the risk of hyperinflation, like in the 1920s in Germany or more recently in Zimbabwe. At the same time they don't dare stop boosting the economy, because that would plunge the economy into a recession and the voters don't like that. In short, the system appears deadlocked. Governments can no longer sustain the illusion they created but neither can they let it go.

So we see that democracy doesn't lead to prosperity, but to ongoing inflation and recessions, with all the uncertainty and instability that come with them. What's the alternative? The solution for the democratic spending spree is to restore respect for private property. If all farmers have their own piece of land, they will make sure no overgrazing occurs. If all citizens can keep the fruits of their own labor, they'll make sure that their resources don't go to waste.

This also means that the financial system must be taken out of the hands of politicians. The monetary system, just like any other economic activity, should become part of the free market again. Everyone should be able to issue their own money or to accept it in any form they like. The mechanisms of the free market will then ensure that no more bubbles are created – at least not of the size we have experienced through government manipulation of our financial system.

For many people such a free-market monetary system may sound frightening. But historically it was the rule rather than the exception. And it might help to realize that our prosperity – the fantastic wealth we currently enjoy – ultimately consists of nothing else than what we together as productive citizens produce and have produced in the form of real goods and services. No more, no less. All the tricks and mirages our democratic governments engage in with their paper money cannot change that fact.

Myth 6
Democracy is necessary to ensure a fair distribution of wealth and help the poor

But isn't democracy necessary to ensure a fair distribution of wealth? Politicians often talk of solidarity and fair sharing of course, but how fair are their schemes really? To begin with, before wealth can be distributed, it must be produced. Government subsidies and services are not free, although many people seem to think so. Roughly half of what is earned by productive people, is taken by the Government and then redistributed.

But let's assume that the State ought to redistribute wealth among the citizens, there's still the question whether the democratic system leads to a fair distribution. Does the money go to the people who really need it? If only that were true. Most grants and subsidies go to special interest groups. To give just one example, two-fifths of the EU budget is spent on farm subsidies.

Lobby groups wage an endless struggle for grants, privileges and jobs. Everyone wants to eat at the trough in which the 'public' funds are deposited. In this system, parasitism, favoritism and dependency are encouraged, individual responsibility and self-reliance discouraged. To mention some special interest groups who benefit from these arrangements although they are hardly poor or disadvantaged: development aid agencies, banks, large corporations, farmers, public broadcasting stations, environmental organizations, cultural institutions. They are able to get billions in grants and subsidies because they have direct access to power. The biggest 'net recipients' are of course the civil servants who run the system. They make sure they are indispensable and award themselves fat salaries.

Special interest groups not only profit from government largesse, but also know how to influence legislation to benefit them at the expense of the rest of society. There are

Lobby groups wage an endless struggle for grants, privileges and jobs. Everyone wants to eat at the trough in which the 'public' funds are deposited.

innumerable examples of this. Think of import restrictions and quotas that benefit the agricultural sector, but increase food prices. Or trade unions that, together with politicians, keep minimum wages high, thereby limiting competition in the labor market. This comes at the expense of the least educated, who can't get a job because they cost too much for companies to hire them.

Another example are licensing laws, a smart way to shut out unwelcome competitors. Pharmacists use licensing laws to block competition from drugstores and internet suppliers. The medical profession blocks competition from 'unlicensed' health care providers. A related example is the system of government granted patents and copyrights which existing companies, for example the pharmaceutical industry and the entertainment industry, use to keep newcomers at bay.

But couldn't voters revolt against the special benefits lobby groups enjoy? In theory this is possible. But in practice it rarely happens, because the benefits special privilege groups enjoy far outweigh the cost to individual members of the public. For example, if a pound of sugar is made three cents more expensive because of import duties, that can be very lucrative for domestic sugar producers (and the State), but for individual consumers it is not worth protesting against. Special interest groups are therefore very motivated to preserve those benefits, while the great mass of voters is too busy to bother.

Most people are probably not even aware of the existence of most of these sweet deals. Nevertheless, all such schemes taken together result in significant costs – and thus a lower standard of living – for all of us who don't have lobbyists working for them in Washington or another Capital. Thus democratic politics inevitably degenerates into a redistribution machine with the most influential and best organized clubs profiting at the expense of the rest of us. And needless to say, the system works both ways in the sense that the lobby groups return the favors they get by sponsoring political campaigns.

In our country, the Netherlands, which may be regarded as a typical European democratic welfare state, the Social and Cultural Planning Bureau (a government agency), concluded in a report published in August 2011 that middle income groups profit less from government benefits than both lower and higher income groups. In fact, the researchers found that the highest income groups profit the most from government benefits! Their research applied only to the year 2007, but there is no reason to assume that the results would be different in other years. Higher income groups in the Netherlands profit in particular from subsidies for higher education, child care and arts.

Many people are afraid that if education, health care, public transport, housing, and so on, are left to 'the forces of the free market', the poor won't be able to afford these services. But free markets actually do a pretty good job providing for the poor. Take supermarkets, which provide our most important necessity of life: food. They deliver high-quality products, at low prices, with a multitude of choice. Through innovation and competition, the free market has made it possible for lower-income groups, like blue collar workers and students, to enjoy goods like cars, personal computers, mobile phones, and air travel that were previously only affordable to the rich. If care for the elderly was organized just as supermarkets are, without intervention by the State, wouldn't we see similar results? That way the elderly and their relatives would decide what services they needed and at what price. They would have much more control over the care they receive and what they pay for it.

Wouldn't quality suffer if the State no longer interfered with schools, hospitals and the care sector? Quite the opposite. What would the quality of our food stores be if they were organized like public schools? You can't expect a handful of 'specialists' in Washington DC to effectively manage large and complex sectors such as education and health care. With their endless reforms, edicts, committees, commissions, white papers, directives, guidelines, and cutbacks they produce nothing in the end but more and more bureaucracy.

The real experts are in the schools and hospitals. They know most about their field of expertise and are best able to organize their institutions efficiently. And if they don't do well, they simply won't survive in a free market. For this reason, the quality of education and health care would improve instead of deteriorate without the interference of government. Bureaucracy, waiting lists and overcrowded classrooms would disappear. Just as there are very few dirty supermarkets with bad food, or opticians with waiting periods of half a year in the free market. They would not survive.

Of course there are always some people who are unable to support themselves. Those people need help. But it is not necessary to create the massive redistribution machine of our democratic system to help them. This can be done by private, charitable institutions –– or anyone else who wants to lend a hand. The assumption that we need democracy to help the poor and disadvantaged is a smokescreen for the self-interest of people who profit from the redistribution machine.

Myth 7
Democracy is necessary to live together in harmony

People often think that conflicts can be avoided by making decisions democratically. After all, if everyone only follows their own inclinations, you can't live together in peace, so this argument goes.

This may be true when a group of people has to decide whether to go to the movies or to the beach. But most questions don't need to be decided democratically. In fact, democratic decision-making more often than not engenders conflicts. This is because all kinds of personal and social issues are turned into collective problems in a democracy. By forcing people to abide by democratic decisions, democracy leads to adversarial rather than harmonious relations between people.

For example, it is decided 'democratically' what children must be taught in school, how much money is spent on elderly care, how much on third world aid, whether smoking in bars

Suppose we decided democratically how much and what kind of bread is baked every day? This would lead to endless lobbying, campaigning, wrangling, meetings and protests.

is allowed, which TV stations are subsidized, what medical treatments are covered by Medicaid, how high rents should be, whether women are allowed to wear headscarves, which drugs people are allowed to take, and so on. All these decisions create conflicts and tensions. These conflicts can easily be avoided. Let people make their own choices and take responsibility for the consequences.

Suppose we decided democratically how much and what kind of bread is baked every day? This would lead to endless lobbying, campaigning, wrangling, meetings and protests. The supporters of white bread would come to regard the proponents of whole wheat bread as their political enemies. If the whole wheaters get the majority all bread subsidies will go to whole wheat and white bread might even be prohibited. And vice versa of course.

Democracy is like a bus full of people who must decide together where the driver will go. The progressives vote for San Francisco, the conservatives prefer Dallas, the libertarians want to go to Las Vegas, the Greens want to go to Woodstock and the rest want to go in a thousand more different directions. Eventually the bus arrives at a place where almost no one will want to be. Even if the driver has no self-interest and listens carefully to what the passengers want, he can never satisfy all their wishes. He has only one bus and there are almost as many wishes as there are passengers.

This is also the reason why newcomers in politics who are at first hailed as saviors in the end always disappoint people. No politician can achieve the impossible. 'Yes we can' always ends in 'no we cannot'. Not even the wisest person in the world can fulfill opposing desires.

It's no coincidence that political discussions between people are often so emotional. In fact many people prefer not to talk about politics when they meet socially. This is because they usually hold very different ideas on 'how to live' and in a democracy these views somehow need to be reconciled.

The solution to the problem of the bus is simple. Let people decide for themselves where they want to go and with whom. Let people decide for themselves how they want to live, let them solve their own problems, form their own groups. Let them decide what to do with their bodies, minds and money. A lot of our political 'problems' will disappear like magic.

In a democracy, however, the very opposite happens. The system encourages people to turn their individual preferences into collective goals that everyone must follow. It encourages those who want to go to place X to try to force others in the same direction. One particularly unfortunate consequence of the democratic system is that people are induced to form groups that will necessarily come into conflict with other groups. This is so because only when you are part of a large enough group (or voting bloc) that there is any chance that can turn your ideas into the law of the land. Thus, the old are turned against the young, farmers against city dwellers, immigrants against residents, Christians against Muslims, believers against atheists, employers against employees, and so on. The greater the differences between people, the more acrimonious relations will become. When one group believes that homosexuality is a sin and another calls for more gay role models in schools and educational materials, they will inevitably clash.

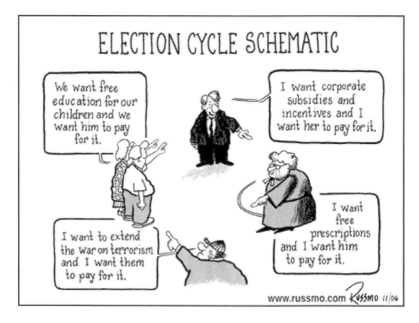

Almost everyone understands that the freedom of religion which evolved centuries ago was a sensible idea that lessened social tensions between religious groups. After all, Catholics could not dictate the lives of Protestants anymore or vice versa. But few people nowadays seem to understand that tensions arise when, through our democratic system, employees can dictate how employers should run their business, elderly can make the young pay for their pensions, banks can make citizens pay for their wrong investments, health freaks can stuff their ideas down other people's throats, and so on.

It also pays to present your group as weak, or disadvantaged, or disenfranchised, or discriminated against. That gives you an extra

> *Enforced solidarity is really a contradiction. Solidarity to be real implies voluntary action.*

argument to ask for government benefits, and it gives the government an argument to justify its existence and to dole out those benefits in the name of 'social justice'.

As the American writer H.L. Mencken said, "What men value in this world is not rights but privileges". This applies to many groups in society and is quite visible in a democracy. Where once women, blacks and homosexuals fought for liberty and equal rights, their modern representatives more often demand privileges like quota, affirmative action and anti-discriminatory laws that limit free speech. They call this rights but since these rights are applicable to only certain groups, they are in reality privileges. Real rights, like the right to free speech, apply to everyone. Privileges only apply to certain groups. They rely on force, because they can only be granted by forcing others to pay for them.

Another tactic to get favors or privileges out of the democratic system is by presenting your cause as necessary to save society from some kind of disaster. If we don't save the climate, or the euro, or the banks, society is doomed, chaos will ensue, millions will suffer. H.L. Mencken saw through this ruse as well. "The urge to save humanity is almost always a false front for the urge to rule", he said. Note that in a democracy people don't have to put their money where their mouth is. They can defend illegal immigrants if they happen to live in a place where they are not bothered by them. They can vote for subsidies for orchestras or museums for which they themselves would not buy expensive tickets, knowing that the costs of the subsidies will be borne by others.

Such people often even display an air of moral superiority. "We don't want to expose art to the free market", proclaims the proponent of art subsidies. What he really means is that *he* does not want this, and that he thinks the rest of society must pay for *his* preference.

'We' is the most abused word in a democracy. Proponents of a measure always say "we want something," "we must do something", "we need something", "we have a right". As if everyone naturally agrees. What they really mean is that *they* want it, but just don't want to take responsibility themselves. People will say "we must help the Third World" or "we must fight in Afghanistan". They never say, "I'm going to help the Third World, who's with me?" or "I'm going to fight against the Taliban." Democracy thus offers a convenient way of shifting personal responsibility to others. By saying 'we' instead of 'I' 99.999% of the burden of a decision is carried by others.

And political parties readily cater to this. They (explicitly or implicitly) promise their constituents that the burden of their favorite goals will be carried by the rest of the people. Thus leftists say, "vote for us, we will take the money away from the rich and give it to you." Rightists tell people, "vote for us, we will finance the war in Afghanistan with money from people who oppose it." All of them tell the farmers, "vote for us, we will ensure that farm subsidies are paid by non-farmers".

Is this a system of goodwill and solidarity, or an antisocial, parasitic system?

The so-called solidarity in a democracy is ultimately based on force. But enforced solidarity is really a contradiction. Solidarity to be real implies voluntary action. You can't say that someone who is robbed on the streets shows solidarity with the robber, no matter how noble the robber's motives.

The fact is that those who use the democratic system to enforce solidarity, can do this because they don't have to pay for it themselves. Note that they never advocate that a similar wealth redistribution should be carried out on a global scale. If sharing with less fortunate people is right, why not broaden welfare schemes to the whole world? Why not create social justice on a global scale? Obviously, the Western advocates of redistribution realize that a global redistribution would lower their income to a few thousand dollar a year. But of course they don't mind 'sharing fairly' with wealthier people.

If you want to give your money away, you don't need to have the majority endorsing this. Freedom is enough. You are free to open your wallet and give what you want. You can donate to a charity or meet up with like-minded people and give together. There is no justification to force the rest of the people to do the same.

Myth 8
Democracy is indispensable to a sense of community

In a democracy, then, every difference in opinion leads to a struggle for power and resources with one group gaining at the expense of others. Everyone makes demands on the State and the State forces other people to meet those demands. It can hardly be otherwise, because the State is after all nothing but an instrument of power that operates by coercion.

The result of this system is that people get spoiled, they demand ever more from their rulers and complain if they don't get their way. At the same time they have little choice but to participate in the system, because if they don't, they will get extorted by the rest of the population. In this way the system undermines people's self-reliance – their ability to fend for themselves. At the same time it undermines people's willingness to help others, since they are already constantly forced to 'help' others.

People's mentality has by now become so 'democratized' that they don't even realize anymore how antisocial their actions and ideas actually are. Nowadays anyone who wants to start up a sports club, a cultural event, a daycare center, an environmental organization, etcetera, tries to get some kind of subsidy first from the local or national government. In other words, they want others to pay for their hobby. Nor is this entirely illogical, because if you don't play this game, you have to pay for other people's hobbies and you get nothing in return. But this system has little to do with the idea of community that people tend to associate with democracy. It's more about survival of the fittest in the struggle for the tax loot.

Ludwig Erhard, former German Chancellor and architect of the postwar German economic miracle, acknowledged this problem of democracy. "How can

A democracy is an organization whose membership is mandatory. A genuine community is based on voluntary participation.

we continue to ensure progress if we increasingly adopt a lifestyle in which nobody is willing to take responsibility for themselves and everyone is looking for safety in collectivism?" he wondered. "If this mania continues, our society will degenerate into a social system in which everyone has their hands in someone else's pockets."

Still, one may ask, wouldn't we lose our national sense of unity if we no longer decided on everything 'together'? It's undoubtedly true that a country is, in a certain sense, a community. There's nothing wrong with that - it can even be a good thing. After all most people aren't loners. They need companionship and they also need each other for economic reasons.

But the question is: is democracy essential for this feeling of unity? It's hard to see why. When you talk about a community, you talk about more than a political system. People share with each other their language, culture and history. Each country has its national heroes, celebrities and sports stars, but also its literature, cultural values, work ethic and lifestyle. None of this is tied to the democratic system. It all existed before there was democracy and there is no reason it cannot continue to exist without democracy.

At the same time, no country has an entirely uniform culture. Within each country there are great differences between people. There are many regional and ethnic communities with strong mutual bonds. And there's nothing wrong with that either. Within the framework of a free society all these social structures and commitments can co-exist. The main point to notice about them is that they are *voluntary.* They are not enforced by the State nor can they be, since cultures and communities are organic entities. You cannot maintain them by government force, and they have little to do with elections.

The difference with these social communities and democracy is that a democracy is an organization whose membership is mandatory. A genuine community is based on voluntary participation. Such a community can have 'democratic' rules of course. The members of a tennis club may decide to vote on who their chairperson will be, how high their membership fees will be, and so on. There's nothing wrong with that. This is a private association and members are free to join or not. If they don't like how their club is run they can join another club or start one themselves. The voluntary nature of the club ensures that it tends to be run well. If, for example, the board were to engage in favoritism, many members would quit. But in our democratic system you don't have the option to leave the club. Democracy is mandatory.

Sometimes people say "Love it or leave it" when they talk about their country. But that implies that the country belongs to the State, to the collective, and that everyone who is accidentally born into it is, by definition, a subject of the State. Even though people were never given a choice.

If someone in Sicily gets extorted by the Mafia, no one says, "Love it or leave it." If a country puts homosexuals in prison people don't say, "they have no cause for complaint, because if they didn't like the rules they should have emigrated." Just as Sicily is not rightfully owned by the Mafia, so too the US (or any other country) is not owned by the majority or the government. Every person owns their own life and should not have to do to what the majority wants. People have a right to do what they want with their lives as long as they don't harm others through violence, theft or fraud. This right is to a large extent denied to them in our national parliamentary democracy.

Myth 9
Democracy equals freedom and tolerance

One of the most persistent myths about democracy is that it is the same as 'freedom'. For many people 'freedom and democracy' belong together like the stars and the moon. But in fact, freedom and democracy are opposites. In a democracy everyone must submit to government decisions. The fact that the government is elected by the majority is irrelevant. Coercion is coercion, whether it is exercised by the majority or by a single ruler.

In our democracy no one can escape the decisions taken by the government. If you don't obey, you will be fined, and if refuse to pay the fine, you will eventually end up in jail. It's as simple as that. Try not paying a traffic ticket. Or your taxes. In this sense there is no fundamental difference between a democracy and a dictatorship. For someone like Aristotle, who lived at a time when democracy had not yet been sanctified, this was obvious. He wrote: "Unlimited democracy is, just like oligarchy, a tyranny spread over a large number of people."

Freedom means that you *don't* have to do what the majority of your fellow men want you to do, but that you can decide for yourself. As the economist John T. Wenders once said, "There is a difference between democracy and freedom. Freedom cannot be measured by the opportunity to vote. It can be measured by the scope of what we do *not* vote about."

That scope is very limited in a democracy. Our democracy hasn't brought us freedom, but the opposite. The government has enacted countless laws that make many voluntary social interactions and relations impossible. Tenants and landlords are not free to make contracts the way they see fit, employers and employees are not free to agree on the wage and labor conditions they wish, doctors and patients are not allowed to freely decide what treatments or drugs they will use, schools are not free to teach what they want, citizens are not allowed to 'discriminate', businesses are not allowed to hire whomever they want, people are not free to take up any profession they want, in many countries political parties must allow female candidates to run for office, educational institutions are subject to racial quotas, and the list goes on. All this has little to do with freedom. Why would people not have the right to come to any kind of contracts or agreements they want? Why do others have a say in agreements to which they are not a party?

Laws that interfere in the freedom of people to enter into voluntary agreements, may benefit certain groups, but they invariably hurt others. Minimum wage laws benefit certain workers, but they hurt people who are less productive than the minimum wage warrants. These people become too expensive to be hired and so they are left unemployed.

Likewise, laws that protect people from getting fired may benefit some people, but they discourage employers from hiring new people. The more rigid the labor laws, the more employers have reason to fear that they get stuck with people whom they cannot get rid of when their business requires them to do so. The result is that they hire as few people as possible, even when times are good. Again, this tends to hurt low-skilled people in particular. At the same time, the resulting high unemployment makes people who do have a job afraid to change career paths.

Similarly, rent control laws benefit existing tenants, but discourage homeowners from renting out housing space and investors from developing real estate projects. Thus these laws lead to housing shortages and drive up rents, hurting people who are looking for a place to live.

Or take laws that dictate minimum standards for products and services. Don't they benefit everyone? Well, no. The downside of these laws is that they limit supplies, reduce consumer choice and raise prices (so, again, they especially hurt the poor). For example, laws mandating safety standards for cars drive up prices and make them unaffordable for the lowest income groups, who are deprived of deciding for themselves what risks they want to take on the road.

To see why such 'protective' regulations have serious drawbacks, imagine that the government would forbid the sale of any car below the quality of a Mercedes Benz. Wouldn't that ensure that we will all be driving the best and safest cars? But of course only those who could afford a Mercedes Benz would still be driving. Or ask yourself: why doesn't the government triple the minimum wage? We would all be making a lot more money, wouldn't we! Well, those who would still have jobs, yes. The others, no. Government cannot perform magic with its laws, even if many people think so.

In a democracy not only do you have to do what the government tells you, for everything you do you basically need permission from the State. In practice individuals are still allowed many freedoms, but the emphasis is on the allowing. All freedoms we have in a democratic nation are granted by the State, and may be taken away from us at any time.

Although nobody asks permission from the government before having a beer, that consent is nonetheless implicitly required. Our democratically elected government can prohibit drinking beer if it wants to. In fact, this did happen of course in the United States during Prohibition. Nowadays you have to be 21 in the US before you are allowed to drink.

Other democratic states have similar rules. In Sweden you can only buy hard liquor in state-owned stores. In many countries and states prostitution is illegal. Norwegian citizens are not even allowed to 'purchase sex' outside Norway. In the Netherlands you need permission from the government to build a shed or change the appearance of your house. Clearly these are all instances of dictatorship, not freedom.

It's sometimes countered that in Western democracies the majority can't just do anything they want or even that democracies in fact typically protect 'minority rights'. That is a myth. Yes, there are currently a few minorities who enjoy special 'protection' from the

State, like feminists, gays and ethnic minorities. Other minorities, such as Mexicans, smokers, drug users, entrepreneurs, squatters, Christians – cannot count on such preferential treatment. The popularity of some minorities has more to do with fashion than with democracy.

The reasons some minorities are left alone or treated preferentially in a democracy are varied. Some are very vocal and immediately take to the streets when their 'rights' (i.e. privileges) are threatened, for example certain public workers, or union workers, or farmers in France. Others are treated gingerly because they are suspected of reacting aggressively when they have to abide by the rules, such as football hooligans, or ethnic gangs, or green activists. If smokers, once a majority, had responded violently to their liberties being trampled upon, many anti-smoking laws would probably not have passed.

> *"There is a difference between democracy and freedom. Freedom cannot be measured by the opportunity to vote. It can be measured by the scope of what we do not vote about."*

The point is, there is nothing in the democratic system itself or in the principle of democracy that guarantees the rights of minorities. The very principle of democracy is precisely that the minority has no inalienable rights. Parliament or Congress can adopt any law they want without taking minorities into account. And fads change. The cuddled minority of today can be the scapegoats of tomorrow.

But don't democracies have Constitutions to protect us against tyrannical legislation by the majority? Up to a point, yes. But note that the US Constitution was adopted before the US was a democracy. And the Constitution can be changed by the democratic system in any way the majority wants – and often has been. Prohibition was approved by a Constitutional Amendment. So was the Income Tax. The very existence of Constitutional Amendments shows that the Constitution is subject to democratic control, i.e. rule of the majority. Nor was the original Constitution perfect. It allowed slavery.

Other democratic countries have Constitutions that are even less protective of individual freedom than the US Constitution. Under the Dutch constitution, the state must provide for jobs, housing, people's livelihoods, health care, the redistribution of wealth, and so on. This Constitution looks more like a social-democratic election program than a manifesto of individual liberty. The European Union has a constitution that says 'it shall work for the sustainable development of Europe based on balanced economic growth and price stability, a highly competitive social market economy, aiming at full employment and social progress, and a high level of protection and improvement of the quality of the environment.' Those and other articles in this document give the European authorities a lot of leeway to regulate people's affairs. Incidentally, the populations of France and The Netherlands voted against this Constitution in referenda, but it was pushed through anyway.

Democracy is also often said to go together with freedom of speech, but again this is a myth. There is nothing in the idea of democracy that favors freedom of speech, as Socrates already found out. Democratic countries have all kinds of rules limiting freedom of speech. In the Netherlands it is forbidden to insult the queen.

In the United States the First Amendment to the Constitution guarantees freedom of speech, but 'with the exception of obscenity, defamation, incitement to riot, and fighting words, as well as harassment, privileged communications, trade secrets, classified material, copyright, patents, military conduct, commercial speech such as advertising, and time, place and manner restrictions'. Those are a lot of exceptions.

The point to note, though, is that the US Constitution – and the freedom of speech that came with it – was adopted before the advent of democracy. The reason people in western democracies enjoy a number of freedoms is not because they are democracies but because they have classical-liberal or libertarian traditions that arose in the 17th and 18th centuries before they became democratic. Many people in these countries do not want to give up these freedoms, even though the spirit of freedom is constantly being eroded by the spirit of democratic meddling.

In other parts of the world people are less attached to personal freedoms. Many non-western democracies show very little respect for individual freedom. In democratic Islamic countries like Pakistan women have little freedom nor is there freedom of speech or freedom of religion. In those countries, democracy is a justification for oppression. If democracy were introduced in absolute monarchies like Dubai, Qatar or Kuwait, this would most likely lead to less freedom rather than more. The Palestinians in the Gaza Strip democratically elected the fundamentalist, not very freedom-loving Hamas (a result which was then, ironically, not accepted by the US and other western democratic governments).

Myth 10
Democracy promotes peace and helps to fight corruption

In the international arena, democratic states are almost by definition the good guys and the others are bad. Democracies are, after all, peace-loving, aren't they? Well, not exactly. All too often democracies show themselves to be pretty warmongering. The United States, the most powerful democracy in the world, started dozens of wars. The American government carried out numerous coups, overthrew governments, supported dictators (Mobutu, Suharto, Pinochet, Marcos, Somoza, Batista, the Shah of Iran, Saddam Hussein, and so on) and dropped bombs on defenseless civilians. Even atomic bombs. Currently, the U.S. has troops in more than 700 military bases in over 100 countries, spending roughly as much on 'defense' as the rest of the world combined.

Democratic Britain invented concentration camps (in South Africa) and was the first to repress nationalist opposition in its colonies through aerial bombardments, destroying entire villages (in Iraq in the 1920s). The democratic British Empire suppressed numerous independence revolts in its colonies, such as in Afghanistan, India and Kenya. Immediately after having been liberated by the Allies from the Nazis, the democratic Netherlands waged a war in Indonesia against people who wanted to be independent. France did the same in Indochina. Democratic countries like Belgium and

France have fought many dirty wars in Africa (e.g. the Belgian Congo and Algeria). The United States is presently still fighting wars in Iraq and Afghanistan which are accompanied by torture and thousands of innocent victims.

A variation of this myth holds that democracies do not wage war *against each other*. Former British Prime Minister Margaret Thatcher said this during a visit to Czechoslovakia in 1990 ("democracies do not go to war with one another") and Bill Clinton said so in a speech to the US Congress in 1994 ("democracies do not attack each other"). This implies that all the wars that democracies have fought were more or less justified because they were not aimed at other democracies, and that, if the whole world were democratic, there would be no more war.

Now it is true that since World War II a large number of 'western' countries - which also happen to be 'democracies' - have been united in NATO and show little tendency to attack each other. But that doesn't mean this has anything to do with democracy or that historically democracies have been peaceful towards each other.

In ancient Greece democratic city-states regularly fought wars against each other. In 1898 the US and Spain fought a war. The First World War was waged against a Germany that was not less democratic than Britain or France. Democratic India and Democratic Pakistan fought several wars since 1947. The United States supported anti-democratic coups against democratically elected governments in Iran, Guatemala and Chile. Israel has waged wars against democratic countries like Lebanon and the Gaza Strip. Democratic Russia recently fought a battle with democratic Georgia.

The reason modern western democracies did not fight wars against each other after the Second World War has to do with very specific historical circumstances,

> *With democratic 'rights' come democratic duties. You have voting rights and therefore a duty to fight for your country's defense.*

on the basis of which it is difficult to draw general conclusions. The most important reason is that they were united in a military alliance, NATO.

There is also a 'law' that holds that "no two countries where a McDonald's restaurant is located ever fought a war against each other." This seemed to have been correct for a long time - until the bombing of Serbia by NATO in 1999 (later counterexamples are the invasion of Lebanon by Israel and the conflict between Russia and Georgia). But it means as little as the statements by Clinton and Thatcher.

One could even argue that democracy has led to an *intensification* of warfare. Before democracy became popular, until the 18th century, kings fought wars with mercenary armies. There was no conscription and the people did not have to fight or hate other nations.

With the rise of democratic-nationalist states this changed. In all democratic countries, general conscription was introduced, starting in France with the French Revolution. The entire population was

51

mobilized to fight wars against the peoples of other countries. Conscripts could easily be used as cannon fodder, as they could be replaced by new conscripts.

It may not seem fair to equate democracy with nationalism, but these two ideologies did become popular simultaneously for a reason. Democracy means government by 'the people'. This notion certainly harbors nationalistic tendencies. With democratic 'rights' come democratic duties. You have voting rights and therefore a duty to fight for your country's defense.

Let's not forget that the disastrous First World War - which paved the way for the totalitarian states of the 20th century and the Second World War — was waged to a large extent by democratic or semi-democratic countries. The First World War took place in Europe after democratic-nationalism had largely pushed back classical liberal thinking.

In the United States too the push for war came from progressive democrats, who began to dominate public opinion at the end of the 19th century. The United States participated in the First World War under the famous slogan of President Wilson "to make the world safe for democracy". If the Americans had remained faithful to the libertarian, 'isolationist' principles of their founding fathers, the US would not have entered the First World War. Then, the war would likely have ended undecided. In that case, the Allies would not have been able to force the burdensome Treaty of Versailles on the Germans, Hitler might never have come to power and World War II and the Holocaust would not have happened.

Democracy does not necessarily bring more 'transparency' or accountability either, as is often claimed. Indeed, the fact that politicians need votes to be elected encourages corruption. They need to do something for their constituents to win votes. This kind of corruption is particularly widespread in the United States, the country of pork barrel politics. American politicians often stop at nothing to win federal funds or programs for their State or district. Furthermore, they tend to be pawns of powerful lobbying organizations, who provide them with the money for their costly electoral campaigns. In addition, the 'revolving doors' of Washington have become notorious, with powerful people switching from politics to business (or the military) and back again without any compunction.

Other democratic countries display similar forms of corruption. In developing countries, democracy almost always go hand in hand with corruption. The same goes for countries like Russia, Italy, France and Greece. Corruption is almost inevitable wherever the State has a lot of power, whatever the political system, and that certainly includes democracy.

Myth 11
People get what they want in a democracy

The basic idea behind democracy is that the people get what they want. Or at least, what the majority wants. In other words, we may complain about the results of our democratic system, but ultimately what we have now is what we wanted, because it's what we democratically chose.

That sounds good in theory, but the reality is different. For example, we can assume that everyone is in favor of better education. Yet we're not getting better education. What we get is harassed teachers, violence in schools, schools as learning factories, students who are no longer able to read, write and do arithmetic. But not better education.

How can this be? It's not because of a lack of democracy; on the contrary, it is the result of how the democratic system works. The fact that education is managed through the democratic system means that politicians and bureaucrats dictate how education is organized and how much money is spent on it. It means that the role of parents, teachers and students to choose for themselves is minimized. State intervention means that schools and universities are inundated with plans, requirements, rules and regulations from the Department of Education. This bureaucratization makes education not better but worse.

When people then complain about the quality of education, politicians respond by implementing even more regulation. What else can they do? The idea that they should end their interference does not enter the minds of politicians and bureaucrats. If they stopped meddling, they would implicitly admit that they are superfluous or even counterproductive, which they will never do of course. It is not in their interest.

The new regulations make the problems worse, because they further restrict the role of students, parents and teachers. They also lead to more bureaucracy and often create perverse

> *In a sense the free market is more 'democratic' than democracy because citizens can make their own choices rather than having the government choose for them.*

incentives. For example, in the Netherlands schools were required by bureaucrats to teach a minimum number of hours, ostensibly to ensure the quality of the education. But this did nothing about the shortage of teachers the schools suffered from, so schools were led to keep pupils sitting in the classroom doing nothing for hours. That the government would try to manage by numbers is not surprising. From a distance the only thing you can measure is quantity. Quality is seen only by those directly involved.

The democratic system can be compared to the state factories in the former Soviet Union. These were centrally controlled and managed on the basis of numbers. Despite (or rather because of) all the attention they got from the State, the quality of production was poor. No communist car could compete with Western models. This was because production was controlled by bureaucrats, not consumers. How can bureaucrats know what consumers want? And what incentives do they have to improve?

The central planning in the Soviet Union brought little technological or cultural innovation. How many inventions were made in communist countries? Quality and innovation are the result of competition and choice, not of central control and state coercion. If private companies want to survive, they must compete by lowering their prices as much as possible, or through innovation or better quality or better service. State-owned enterprises have no such incentive, as they are backed by government-money.

Because our educational system is (partially) organized through the democratic system, it is (to that extent) a state product, making it similar to the state-owned factories in the Soviet Union. Incidentally, this example shows how democracy inevitably leads to a degree of socialism. The free market doesn't operate by democratic processes. Yet in a sense the free market is more 'democratic' than democracy because citizens can make their own choices rather than having the government choose for them.

What applies to education also applies to other sectors that are democratically controlled, such as health care and crime control. Most people want better

> *Politicians always offer the same solution: Give us more money and more power and we will fix the problems.*

protection against crime. Yet democracy does not deliver what the people want. People vote for politicians who promise to combat crime, but the result is usually only more insecurity and crime instead of less.

In the Netherlands crime per capita increased six fold between 1961 and 2001 and every year 700,000 reported criminal offences remain uninvestigated. In many of these cases (at least 100,000), the police know the offender, but they don't follow up the case because they lack the time or just don't care. Police officers have to spend most of their time on paper work. Still, they do find the time to shut down weed plantations and book people for minor traffic violations.

The poor performance of the police is the direct result of the fact that it is democratically controlled. The police has been granted a monopoly in law enforcement. Everybody understands that if ExxonMobil was granted a monopoly in the oil market, the price of gasoline would rise and service would plummet. The same applies to the police. The police are an organization that receives *more* money the *fewer* the number of criminals they catch. If the police were successful in reducing crime their budget would be cut and police officers would lose their jobs. The same applies to all government organizations. You can't even blame the people who work in this system. Only the most diligent and most morally upright would behave differently, given the perverse incentives of the system.

Although the police are not very good at catching criminals, they are very skilled at one thing: filling out forms. Anyone who ever has reported a crime can testify to this. You can hardly blame them –

> *The fact that education is managed through the democratic system means that politicians and bureaucrats dictate how education is organized and how much money is spent on it.*

they are constantly bombarded with new rules they must comply with. In the Netherlands, of the 7000 additional police officers who started work between 2005 and 2009, only 127 ended up being active on the streets doing their job. According to the police, this was the result of the huge bureaucratic workload created by government regulations.

To make matters worse, police are getting ever more – rather than fewer – powers. This is particularly true in the US, after the 9/11 attacks, where law enforcement organizations have been given ever more – dubious – powers, such as preventive body searches at airports, the right to place phone taps, torture terrorist suspects and disregard judicial protections of citizens that used to be taken for granted in our legal system, such as habeas corpus.

Is there an alternative to the top-down security that is forced upon us? Certainly. The alternative is that individuals, businesses, neighborhoods and cities get more control over their own security. The monopoly of the police should give way to competition among security firms. People should no longer be forced to pay taxes for government police and be allowed to hire private security firms. This would lower prices and increase quality. Even now, the private security sector is growing apace, as people increasingly realize they cannot rely on the police for protection.

What goes for education and the police, also goes for other 'public' sectors, such as health care. Again, here democratic control leads to low quality and high cost. One can only begin to imagine the innovation that would occur in health care if it really became part of the free market.

The fact is that people usually don't get what they want in a democracy. The democratic one-size-fits-all principle, leads to centralization, bureaucracy and monopolization (the characteristics of socialism). It inevitably leads to poor quality and high costs.

If you need proof that democracy does not live up to its promises, consider that at every election politicians admit that government has made a mess of things. Every time they promise they will change everything – education, safety, health care, and so on – for the better. But they always offer the same solution: Give us more money and more power and we will fix the problems. This never happens, of course, because the problems are caused by the money and the power of those same politicians.

Myth 12
We are all democrats

If democracy fails to deliver what people actually want, how is it that most people still support it? Because isn't every right-thinking citizen a democrat, even though he may sometimes grumble about the government?

Well, the latter is debatable. Whether people really believe in something, depends not on what they *say* but on what they *do* when they have a free choice. If someone is forced to eat chicken every day and he says he loves chicken, that's not very convincing. It's only credible if he is free not to eat chicken. The same goes for democracy. Democracy is compulsory. Everyone has to participate in it. Individuals, towns, cities, counties, states they all must submit themselves and no one can 'secede'. Would people move to another city, 20 miles away, if taxes there were lower and bureaucracy less intrusive, even if they were not allowed to vote there? Many probably would. Many people already vote with their feet and move to prosperous regions in the world where there's little or no democracy.

Someone in a democracy who says he's in favor of democracy sounds like a citizen of the former Soviet Union who says he would choose a Lada even if he had the chance to buy a Chevrolet or Volkswagen. Could be, but not likely. Like the Soviet citizen who had no choice but Lada, we have no choice but democracy.

In fact, many right-minded democrats would no doubt be happy to escape the measures which they have supposedly chosen through the ballot box. If they had a choice. would people really voluntarily pay their social security tax to the government, not knowing whether social security benefits are still around by the time they retire? How many low-quality, high-priced government services would they choose to pay for voluntarily if they had a choice to spend their money any way they wished?

The American economist Walter Williams recognized the fact that generally we don't want our individual decisions to become democratic decisions. He wrote: "To highlight the offensiveness to liberty that democracy and majority rule is, just ask yourself how many decisions in your life would you like to be made democratically. How about what car you drive, where you live, whom you marry, whether you have turkey or ham for Thanksgiving dinner? If those decisions were made through a democratic process, the average person would see it as tyranny and not personal liberty. Isn't it no less tyranny for the democratic process to determine whether you purchase health insurance or set aside money for retirement? Both for ourselves, and our fellow man around the globe, we should be advocating liberty, not the democracy that we've become where a roguish Congress does anything upon which they can muster a majority vote."

The fact that many supporters of democracy don't really believe in the ideas they promote, can be seen in the hypocritical behavior of democratic politicians and government officials, who only too often don't practice what they preach. Think of socialist politicians who criticize the high salaries of business executives and then join corporations when they retire from politics. Or politicians who preach the blessings of multiculturalism but live in white neighborhoods and send their children to white schools. Or politicians who vote for wars but would never send their own children to fight in them.

There are several reasons why people claim to support democracy, even though their behavior shows the opposite. First, it is understandable that people attribute our relative prosperity to the

Democracy is compulsory. Everyone has to participate in it. Individuals, towns, cities, counties, states they all must submit themselves and no one can 'secede'.

political system we live under. We are pretty well off, and we live in a democracy, so democracy must be a good system, so their reasoning goes. But this is fallacious. Compare this to what some apologists for the Soviet Union said about Lenin and Stalin. Sure, these dictators may have committed atrocities, but people should nonetheless be grateful to them, because under their rule the Soviet Union was industrialized and everyone was supplied with electricity. But Russia would have been 'electrified' and industrialized anyway in the 20th century, even if Lenin and Stalin had never been around. Similarly, the progress we have made in our society cannot simply be attributed to our political system. Look at China. The Chinese economy has grown at breakneck speed, but the country has no democracy. Prosperity is based on the degree of economic freedom people enjoy and the security of their property rights, not on the degree of democracy.

A second reason people tend to support our system, is that they find it difficult to imagine what their lives would be like if they could keep all the money they earned and didn't have to pay taxes. You can see the "free" public highway that you drive on, but you can't see the new health care center that could have been built with the same money. Nor can you imagine the vacation you could have had, if you had not had to pay for the war in Iraq. Even less visible is the innovation that would occur if government didn't interfere in the economy. In a free market, many new and lifesaving medical treatments would undoubtedly have been developed, which are now smothered by bureaucracy.

It often looks as if the government magically provides many things for free, but there is a hidden price to be paid: all possibilities – services, products, innovations – that are *not* created because the means to do so have been usurped by the State. People only see what is conjured out of the government hat, not what disappears into it.

And then there is a third reason why we all think that we are all democrats, namely because we are continuously being told we are. Our schools, the media, politicians, they all constantly give out the message that the only possible alternative to democracy is dictatorship. Given this godly status, as a bulwark against evil, who would dare to be against democracy?

Myth 13
There is no (better) alternative

If you say you're against democracy, people immediately suspect you're in favor of dictatorship. But that's nonsense. Dictatorship is not the only alternative to democracy. The alternative to buying a car democratically is not a dictator buying the car for you but you buying it for yourself.

Winston Churchill said: "Democracy is the worst form of government except for all the others that have been tried". In other words, democracy has its drawbacks, but there is no better system. In his famous book 'The End of History and the Last Man' Francis Fukuyama even wrote about "the universalization of Western liberal democracy as the final form of human government." Presumably, something better could never exist.

In this way, any criticism of democracy is conveniently nipped in the bud. Democracy supposedly stands 'above the political parties and ideologies', and because of that heavenly status a different or better alternative is unimaginable. But this is pure propaganda. Democracy is a specific form of political organization. There is no reason to presume that it is necessarily the best ordering principle. We don't use democracy in the scientific realm, we don't vote about scientific truth, but we use logic and facts, and for good reason. So there is no reason to assume democracy is necessary the best system in the political realm.

Why couldn't people organize themselves differently than in a nation-state in which 'the people' rule? In smaller communities, for example? But

> *The alternative to buying a car democratically is not a dictator buying the car for you but you buying it for yourself.*

decentralization is strongly opposed by our democratic rulers and even made impossible. If democracy really is such a good system, you would expect people to be given the option to voluntarily join – or secede from – a democratic nation. Given the blessings of democracy, surely most people would stand in line to join? But this is not the case. In no democratic country, including the US, are states or regions allowed to go their own separate way.

In fact, the trend in democratic countries is rather the opposite, towards more and more centralization. Europe for one is gradually turning into a democratic Super State. With the dubious result that now the Germans can decide how the Greeks should live and vice versa. In this mega-democracy countries are able to burden the residents of other countries with the consequences of their own short-sighted economic policies – just like citizens in a national democracy can live off the backs of their fellow citizens. Some countries waste money - they don't save, pamper their civil servants with generous pension schemes, create debts that they can never pay off – and if they can get enough other EU countries to agree, they can force the taxpayers of better run countries to pay the bill. That is the logic of democracy at the European level.

The bigger a democratic state is, and the more heterogeneous the population, the greater the tensions that will arise. The various groups in such a state will have little hesitation to use the democratic process to plunder from and interfere with other people as much as possible for their own gain. The smaller the administrative units, and the more homogeneous the population, the greater the chance that the excesses of democracy remain limited. People who know each other personally or feel related to each other, will be less likely to rob and oppress each other.

For this reason it would be a good idea to give people the option of 'administrative secession'. If New Hampshire were allowed to secede from the US, it would have much more freedom to organize things differently than is done, say, in California. It could implement its own tax system that could be favorable to entrepreneurs and employees alike. Regions would compete with each other and laws would be brought more in line with what people want. People could 'vote' with their feet by moving to a different state. Governance would become much more dynamic and less bureaucratic. Regions could learn from each other because they could each experiment with different policies.

Welfare for the poor, for example, can be organized much better at a local level. Local control prevents misuse and is the best guarantee that those who really need help are helped and money is not wasted on freeloaders. The dismantling of the national-democratic welfare state is also important for a successful integration of minorities. Now, many immigrants just live off the welfare state. Those are the immigrants that no one wants. But most people don't mind immigrants who can take care of themselves and are willing to blend in.

By the way, Churchill also said: "The best argument against democracy is a five-minute conversation with the average voter".

II. The crisis of democracy

Democracy may have started out as a great ideal to empower the people, but after 150 years of practice, the results are in, and they are not positive. It is clear now that democracy is a tyrannical rather than a liberating force. Western democracies have followed the path of the socialist countries and have become stagnant, corrupt, oppressive and bureaucratized. As we have tried to show above, this has happened not because the democratic ideal was subverted, but, on the contrary, because of the inherently collectivist nature of the ideal.

If you want to know how democracy really works, consider this example. George Papandreou, the Greek Socialist politician, won the elections in his country in 2009 with a simple slogan: THERE IS MONEY! His conservative opponents had reduced the wages of civil servants and other public expenditures. Papandreou said this was not necessary. "Lefta yparchoun" was his rallying cry – there is money. He won the elections easily. In reality there was no money of course – or rather, the money had to be supplied from taxpayers in other countries in the European Union. But the majority is always right in a democracy, and when they discover they can vote riches for themselves, they will inevitably do so. To expect them to do otherwise is naive.

What the Greek example also shows is that people in a democracy naturally turn to the State to take care of them. Democratic rule means rule by the State. As a result, people will continually make demands upon the State. They will become more and more dependent on the government to solve their problems and run their lives. Whatever problem they encounter, they expect the government to fix it. Obesity, drug abuse, unemployment, a shortage of teachers or nurses, a drop in museum visits, you name it, the State is there to do something about it. Whatever happens – a fire in a theater, an airplane crash, a barroom brawl – they expect the government to go after the culprits and to make sure nothing like this happens again. If they are out of job, they expect the government to "create jobs". If gas prices go up, they want the government to do something about it. On Youtube there is a video that shows an interview with a woman who has just listened to a speech by President Obama, and she is almost crying with joy. She exclaims that "I won't have to worry anymore about paying gas for my car or paying my mortgage!". That's the kind of mentality democracy breeds.

And politicians are quite willing to supply what the people demand of them. They are like the proverbial man who has only a hammer and sees everything as a nail to hit. In the same way, for every problem in society, they see themselves as the problem solver. After all, that's why they are elected. They promise they will 'create jobs', reduce interest rates, boost people's purchasing power, make home ownership affordable for even the poorest, improve education, build playgrounds and sports fields for our children, make sure all products and work places are safe, provide good and affordable health care for everyone, rid the roads of traffic jams, the streets of crime, the neighborhoods of vandalism, defend our 'national' interests in the rest of the world, enforce 'international law' across the globe, promote emancipation and fight discrimination everywhere, make sure the food is safe and the water clean, 'save the climate', make the country the cleanest, greenest and most innovative in the world, and banish hunger from the earth. They will fulfill all our dreams and demands, protect us from our cradles to our graves, make sure we are happy and content from early morning until late at night – and of course cut the budget and reduce taxes.

Such are the dreams democracy is made of.

The sins of democracy

Obviously, in reality this can never work. Government cannot achieve all this. Ultimately, politicians will do the only things they can do, which is:

1. Throw money at problems
2. Make up new rules and regulations
3. Set up committees to supervise implementation of their rules

There is really nothing else they can do, as politicians. They can't even pay the bills for their activities, which are left to the taxpayers to foot.

You can see the consequences of this system around you every day:

Bureaucracy. Democracy has everywhere given birth to large bureaucracies, that rule over our lives with ever more arbitrary power. Since they are the government, they are able to make sure they are well protected from the harsh economic realities that the rest of us are faced with. Their departments can never go broke, they themselves can hardly get fired, and they will seldom run afoul of the law, since they are the law. At the same time, they put a huge burden on the rest of us with their rules and regulations. Everywhere start-up businesses are hindered and discouraged by a multitude of laws and bureaucratic costs that are imposed on them. Existing businesses also suffer under the weight of bureaucracy. In the US the costs of regulation according to the Small Business Administration – notice that this is a government agency – are $1.75 trillion per year, according to an article on Wikipedia. The poor and lowly educated suffer the most from this system: they can't find jobs because they are priced out of the market through minimum wage laws and other laws that drive up labor costs. It's also very difficult for them to set up their own business because they don't know their way around in the bureaucratic jungle.

Parasitism. In addition to the bureaucrats and politicians, there is another group of people that do very well by the democratic system: those who run the companies and institutions that owe their existence to government largesse or special privileges. Think of the managers of companies in the military-industrial complex, and of the banks and financial institutions that are propped up by the Federal Reserve System. But also the people in the "subsidized sectors" – cultural institutions, public television, aid agencies, environmental groups, and so on – not to mention the whole circus of 'international institutions'. A lot of these people have lucrative jobs that they owe to their intimate connections with government or government agencies. This is a form of institutionalized parasitism aided and abetted by our democratic system.

Megalomania. Frustrated by their inability to really change society, the government regularly launches megaprojects to help recover a failing industrial sector or to serve some other noble purpose. Invariably such actions only increase the problems and they always cost much more than planned. Think of educational reforms, health care reform plans, infrastructure projects and energy boondoggles such as the ethanol program in the US or the offshore wind power projects in Europe. Wars too may be seen as 'public projects' undertaken by the government to divert attention from domestic problems, whip up public support for the government, create jobs for the underclasses, and direct huge profits to favorite companies which in turn sponsor politicians' election campaigns and have jobs available for those same politicians when they are voted out of office. (Needless to say, the politicians themselves never fight in the wars they start.)

Welfarism. The politicians who are appointed to fight poverty and inequality naturally feel it as their sacred duty to continuously introduce new welfare programs (and new taxes to pay for them). This serves not only their own interests but also those of the bureaucrats in charge of implementing the programs. Welfare now takes up a substantial part of government spending in most democratic countries. In Britain the Government spends a third of its budget on welfare. In Italy and France this figure approaches 40 percent. Many social organizations (e.g. trade unions, public pension funds, government employment agencies) have an interest in preserving and expanding the welfare state. Typical of the way democratic government works is that it offers no choice and does not enter into contracts with its citizens. Everyone is forced to pay high unemployment insurance and social security premiums, but no one knows what benefits they will enjoy in the future. The money they have had to pay has already been spent. The coming social security debacle is the most egregious example of this kind of profligacy. And bear in mind, the welfare does not only go to the 'disadvantaged'. A lot of 'welfare' goes to the rich, for example to the banks that were bailed out to the tune of $700 billion (after which executives awarded themselves handsome bonuses).

Antisocial behavior and crime. The democratic welfare state encourages irresponsibility and antisocial behavior. In a free society people who misbehave themselves, fail to keep their promises, or act without concern for others, forfeit the help of friends, neighborhood and family. However, our welfare state tells them: If nobody wants to help you anymore, we will! Thus people are rewarded for antisocial behavior. As they are used to the government providing everything they need, they develop the mentality of freeloaders, who don't want to work for their money. To make matters worse, rigid labor laws (as well as anti-discrimination laws) make it hard for employers to get rid of employees who don't perform satisfactorily. Similarly, government regulations make it almost impossible to expel students or fire teachers who misbehave or underperform. In public housing projects it's very difficult to evict someone from his house who is a nuisance to his neighbors. Groups that misbehave themselves in nightspots cannot be refused entry because of anti-discrimination laws. To add insult to injury, the government often sets up expensive assistance programs for antisocial groups, like soccer hooligans. Thus, delinquency is rewarded and encouraged.

Mediocrity and lower standards. Since the majority in any society tend to be poorer than the more successful and competent members of society, there is inevitably pressure on politicians in

> *The main drive for politicians in a democracy is the desire to be re-elected. Therefore, their horizon usually does not reach beyond the coming elections.*

a democracy to redistribute wealth – to take from the rich and give to the poor. In this way, business success and excellence are punished through progressive taxes. Thus, democracy may be expected to lead to a dumbing down of the population and a lowering of general cultural standards. Where the majority rules, the average becomes the norm.

Culture of discontent. Private disagreements are continually turned into social conflicts in a democracy. This is because the State interferes with all personal and social relations. Everything that goes wrong somewhere, from a poorly functioning public school to a local riot, balloons into a nationwide (or even international) issue for which politicians have to find a solution. Everyone feels impelled and encouraged to force their worldview on others. Groups who feel wronged throw up blockades, organize protests or go on strike. This creates a general feeling of frustration and discontent.

Short term-ism. The main drive for politicians in a democracy is the desire to be re-elected. Therefore, their horizon usually does not reach beyond the coming elections. Additionally, democratically elected politicians work with resources that are not theirs and which are only temporarily at their disposal. They spend other people's money. That means they don't have to be careful about what they do and think about the future. For these reasons short-term policies prevail in a democracy. One former Dutch Minister of Social Affairs once said, "Political leaders should govern as if there were no elections anymore. That way they would they be able to take the long-term view of things." But that is precisely what they can't do of course. As the American author Fareed Zakaria put it in an interview: "I think we face a real crisis in the western world. What you see is the fundamental inability in every western society to do one thing, which is to impose any kind of short term pain for long term gain. Whenever a government tries to propose some kind of pain there is a revolt. And the revolt is almost always successful." Since people are encouraged to behave like freeloaders in a democracy and politicians behave more like tenants than property owners, as they are just temporarily in office, this result should surprise no one. Someone who rents or leases something has far less incentive to be careful with it and think long-term than an owner.

Private disagreements are continually turned into social conflicts in a democracy. This is because the State interferes with all personal and social relations.

Why things keep getting worse

In theory people could vote for a different, less bureaucratic and less wasteful system. In practice, this is not likely to happen, as there are too many people who acquire a vested interest in preserving the system. And as government slowly grows bigger, this group grows with it. As the great Austrian economist Ludwig von Mises pointed out, the bureaucracy in particular will resist any kind of change tooth and nail. "The bureaucrat is not only a government employee", Mises wrote. "He is, under a democratic constitution, at the same time a voter and as such a part of the sovereign, his employer. He is in a peculiar position: he is both employer and employee. And his pecuniary interest as employee towers above his interest as employer, as he gets much more from the public funds than he contributes to them. This double relationship becomes more important as the people on the government's payroll increase. The bureaucrat as voter is more eager to get a raise than to keep the budget balanced. His main concern is to swell the payroll."

Economist Milton Friedman divided money spending into four types. The first is when you spend your money on yourself. You have an incentive to look for

> *Governments spend someone else's money on someone else. So they have no reason to care about quality or cost.*

quality and to spend efficiently. This is generally how money is spent in the private sector. The second type is spending your money on someone else, for instance when buying someone dinner. You certainly care about the amount you spend but are less interested in quality. The third type is when you spend someone else's money on yourself, such as when you have lunch on your company's expense account. You will experience little incentive to be frugal but you will make an effort to pick the right lunch. The fourth way is to spend someone else's money on someone else. Then you have no reason to care about quality or cost. That is generally how government spends your tax money.

Politicians are rarely held accountable for the measures they have implemented and that turn out to be harmful in the long run. They get kudos for their good intentions and the initial positive results of their programs. The long-term negative consequences (for example, debts that need to be repaid) will be the responsibility of their successors. Conversely, politicians have little incentive to work on programs that will lead to results after they have left office, because these will be credited to future leaders.

Thus, democratic governments invariably spend more money than they receive. They solve this problem by raising taxes, or even better – since taxes tend to be resented by people who have to pay them – by borrowing money or simply printing it. (Note that they tend to borrow from favorite banks, which then get bailed out by the government if they get in debt too much.) They rarely cut their own budget. When they talk about "cutting back", they usually mean a slower *growth* of spending.

Printing money of course leads to inflation, which implies a constant decrease in the value of people's savings. Borrowing money causes the national debt to rise and leads to interest payments for future generations. Currently, the public debts of almost all democracies in the world have become so high that they are not likely ever to be repaid. What is worse is that institutions like pension funds have massively bought government debt under the assumption that this would be a good long-term investment. That's a cruel joke. Many people will never receive the pension they counted on because the money they put in their pension funds has already been squandered.

Yet despite all these problems that democracy brings us, we continue to hope and believe that, after the next elections, everything will change. This leaves us stuck in a vicious circle: The system doesn't deliver what it promises, people become frustrated and demand improvement, politicians crank up their promises even further, expectations get even higher, the inevitable disappointments get even bigger, and so on. Citizens in a democracy are like alcoholics who need to drink ever more to get intoxicated, each time resulting in an even bigger hangover. Instead of concluding that they should stay off the liquor, they only want more. They have totally forgotten how to take care of themselves and are no longer in charge of their own lives.

Why we need less democracy

The question is how long this situation can continue, given the discontent in society and the instability of the political and economic system. Many people realize that there is something wrong with the system. Politicians and opinion leaders bemoan the fragmentation of the political landscape, the fickleness of the electorate, the superficiality and sensationalism of the media. Citizens complain that politicians don't listen to them, that they don't get what they are promised and that Congress is a charade, a mockery of good government. However, they blame the problems on the wrong politicians or on side issues such as immigration or globalization, not on the deficiencies inherent in the democratic system itself.

Right now nobody really knows where to go from here. Everyone is stuck in the tunnel vision called democracy. The only 'solution' that people can think of is 'more

> *Citizens in a democracy are like alcoholics who need to drink ever more to get intoxicated, each time resulting in an even bigger hangover.*

democracy', i.e. more government intervention. Are young people drinking too much alcohol? Raise the drinking age! Are the chronically ill neglected in nursing homes? Send in more government inspectors! Is there a lack of innovation? Install a government Innovation Board! Do children learn too little at school? Mandate more tests! Is crime on the increase? Set up a new government department! Regulate, forbid, force, discourage, check, inspect, pamper, reform and, above all, throw money at the problem.

And what if it all won't work? Eventually the call for a Great Leader will be heard, a strong man to put an end to all the cackling and will deliver Law and Order. There is a certain logic to this. If everything needs to be regulated by the State, then why not have it done properly by a benevolent dictator? Away with the endless dithering, the indecisiveness, the quarreling, the inefficiency. But this would be a devil's bargain. We would get law and order, that's true. But the price would be an end to freedom, dynamism and growth.

Fortunately, there is another way, even though many people may find it hard to imagine. The way is: Less democracy. Less State. More individual freedom.

How this libertarian ideal might look in practice, is the subject of the last chapter of this book.

III. Towards a new political ideal

It's an illusion to think that the problems our society faces can be resolved with 'more democracy'. Let alone that democracy is the best of all possible systems.

Democracy originated at a time when government was relatively small. A century and a half of democracy, however, has led to a tremendous expansion of the State in all democratic countries. It has also led to the situation where we should not only fear the State but also our fellow-citizens who are able to enslave us through the ballot box.

The blind belief in democracy in our society is not self-evident. It is in fact a fairly recent phenomenon. It may come as a surprise to many readers, but the great founding fathers of the United States – men like Benjamin Franklin, Thomas Jefferson and John Adams – were without exception opposed to democracy. "Democracy," said Benjamin Franklin, "is two wolves and a lamb voting on what they are going to have for lunch. "Liberty," he added, "is a well-armed lamb contesting the vote." Thomas Jefferson said that democracy "is nothing more than mob rule, where 51% of the people may take away the rights of the other 49%."

They were hardly alone. Most classical-liberal and conservative intellectuals in the 18th and 19th Century, including famous thinkers such as Lord Acton, Alexis de Tocqueville, Walter Bagehot, Edmund Burke, James Fenimoore Cooper, John Stuart Mill and Thomas Macaulay, were opposed to democracy. The famous conservative writer Edmund Burke wrote: "Of this I am certain, that in a democracy the majority of the citizens is capable of exercising the most cruel oppression upon the minority … and that oppression of the minority will extend to far greater numbers and will be carried on with much greater fury, that can almost ever be apprehended from the dominion of a single sceptre."

Thomas Macalauy, the famous British liberal thinker, expressed similar sentiments: "I have been long convinced that institutions purely democratic must sooner or later destroy liberty, or civilization, or both." These were perfectly acceptable ideas in those days, as Erik Ritter von Kuehnelt-Leddihn shows in his book "Liberty or Equality" (1951).

During the late 19th and 20th Century, however, the classical liberal ideal was increasingly pushed into the background and replaced by faith in collectivism – the notion that the individual is subordinate to the group. Liberalism was replaced by various forms of collectivism – communism, socialism, fascism and democracy. The latter now passes for our idea of 'freedom'. But as we have shown in this book, it's totally false to equate democracy with freedom. As classical-liberal thinkers in the past recognized, democracy is in fact a – quite clever – form of socialism. What is left of our liberty, is due to the classical liberal tradition that is still alive in the west, not to democracy.

This classical-liberal tradition, however, is under heavy pressure. With each new generation that grows up with the daily democratic propaganda that is all around us, a part of our liberal heritage dies off. Nobody is surprised anymore when women demand quotas on the boards of companies, when the State prohibits smoking in pubs or when the government decides what our children are taught in school. Not everyone may agree with these notions – but everyone finds it perfectly normal that the government should decide on such matters. There is hardly any opposition to the fact that we live under a system that interferes with our lives down to the smallest detail. There is no principled opposition to the notion that it should be decided 'democratically' how we all should live.

Decentralization and individual liberty

Is an alternative to democracy possible? A society without an overriding State, without majoritarian rule, a free and cooperative society?

Absolutely. Such an alternative is urgently needed if we do not want to slide into tyranny and stagnation. The Western world needs a new ideal. An ideal that combines dynamism and individual freedom with social harmony.

74

Such an ideal is not Utopian. It can be achieved. The first thing that has to be done is to reduce the role of government. People need to regain control over their lives and the fruits of their labor. Without meddlesome rules and taxation people will create safe, liveable and sustainable communities. Why can't people spend their own money as they wish and buy the insurance, health care and education they choose? What great disaster would befall us if that were to happen? Why should the State take people's money through taxes and make those decisions for them? People must again be given the freedom to choose for themselves, to solve their problems as they see fit – individually or, probably more often, together. For without cooperation, order and prosperity are impossible. But cooperation can only really work on a voluntary basis, based on mutual consent.

People must regain control over the fruits of their own labor. They must have the freedom to create their own local – religious, communist, capitalist, ethnic, and so on – communities. These

> *Why not a market for governance, where governments have to compete, and where citizens can easily move to another government area to live and work?*

might be governed 'democratically', if the residents want to, or not, if they do not.

A market for governance

Patri Friedman, grandson of Nobel laureate Milton Friedman, once said: "Government is a sector with a very high barrier to entry. In fact, you must win the election or start a revolution to try a new form of government."

There is indeed little choice and competition in government. People consider it important that companies compete. People expect a flexible free market in cars, clothing and insurance with many different suppliers. Then why not a market for governance, where governments have to compete, and where citizens can easily move to another government area to live and work? Currently people can move to another city, but because most taxes and laws come from the federal government, this does not change anything. To obtain a different kind of governance, people are forced to emigrate, which is an enormous barrier.

We know that companies have a tendency to form monopolies and cartels, in order to reduce competition. But governments have that tendency as well. Look at the concentration of government power in Washington or Brussels. In a free market, however, it is always possible for people to start new businesses, to challenge existing monopolies and cartels. That is why monopolies tend to be short-lived in the private sector. When monopolists ask high prices or abuse their market position, it encourages other companies to enter that particular market.

In governance such competition is lacking. Like true monopolists politicians do not want competition in governance. They prefer

> *Decentralization, unlike national democracy, is a system of 'live and let live'.*

that all matters are decided upon collectively at a central level. "Illegal immigration can only be solved in a European context," they will say. Or: "The debt crisis can only be tackled internationally." Or: "Terrorism can only be fought through a powerful central agency." However, there are many small countries in the world that are not part of 'blocs' and that do not suffer from economic crises or terrorism. Similarly we are supposed to believe that education, health care, finance, social insurance, and so on, have to be coordinated and regulated at least at a national level. But there's no reason why this should be so.

Decentralization would be beneficial to many groups in society. With local autonomy, progressive thinkers can bring their progressive ideas into practice and conservative thinkers can do the same with their values, without forcing others to adjust to their way of life. People who would like to start an eco-hippie community can live according to their dreams. At their own expense of course. A religious community that wants to keep its shops closed on Sunday can do so. One size fits all is unnecessary and unwanted.

Decentralization, unlike national democracy, is a system of 'live and let live'. So let a thousand nations bloom.

Diversity in governance implies that people can decide more easily under what system they wish to live. They can go to another municipality or county if they desire different governance. Such competition ensures that rulers are held accountable, which is hardly the case when a citizen's influence is restricted to elections once every four years. Even when only few citizens actually move to another area, there will be a strong incentive for rulers to improve their policies.

If not everything is centrally determined, regions can choose a direction that suits their circumstances and preferences. For instance, a particular area can choose to greatly reduce taxes and regulation in order to stimulate economic activity. The American historian Thomas E. Woods points out that political freedom arose in Western Europe precisely because of the fragmentation and differentiation that reigned there historically. A multitude of small jurisdictions made it possible for people to flee from places where oppression reigned to more liberal places. Tyrannical rulers thus found themselves forced to allow more freedom.

Decentralization in Switzerland

Switzerland has long proven that decentralization can work fine. People often think that size and centralization bring prosperity and all sorts of other benefits. However, Switzerland, which is neither a member of the EU nor of NATO, proves otherwise. With almost 8 million inhabitants this country has about the population of Virginia and its governance is highly decentralized. 26 cantons – counties - compete with each other and enjoy a great deal of autonomy. The cantons were once separate autonomous states, and some have fewer than 50,000 inhabitants. In addition there are some 2900 municipalities in Switzerland - the smallest has about thirty inhabitants. This is a lot more than most other European countries. The major part of Swiss income taxes is paid to the municipality and the canton, not to the federal government. The municipalities and cantons differ greatly in taxation and regulation and thus compete for the favors of citizens and companies.

It is well-known of course that Switzerland is a highly successful country. It is in the top league of the world in terms of life expectancy, employment, well-being and prosperity. It is one of the few countries in the world that hasn't experienced war for over a century. Despite the existence of four languages (German, French, Italian and Romansh), there is a great deal of social harmony, in stark contrast with the situation in Belgium where the tensions and conflicting interests between the Dutch speaking Flemish and the French speaking Walloons are always threatening to split the country. Whereas the Flemish complain that they have to pay for the less wealthy Walloons, the Swiss do not experience such friction because of their decentralized system.

Of course, Switzerland is a democracy, but the country has so many and such small democratic units, that it manages to avoid many of the negative effects of national parliamentary democracy.

Switzerland also shows how the possibility of secession reduces tensions. In the 1970s the French speaking inhabitants of the canton of Bern felt not well represented in the predominantly German-speaking area in which they live. So in 1979 the French-speaking communities seceded and formed the canton of Jura. Throughout the centuries, disputes between different ethnic and language groups have been peacefully resolved in that way. As Swiss cantons and communities are small, the people cannot only vote at the ballot box, but also have the choice to move if they are dissatisfied with the governance. This way, bad policies are driven out by good policies.

This does not mean we advocate the Swiss model as an ideal or the only option. But it is an example that shows how decentralized governance could work and how it leads to lower taxes and greater individual liberty. Nor do we mean that democracy is necessarily a good thing as long as it is kept small. A democracy with three people is still wrong if no one can escape from it. Then it can have the same negative effects as a democracy with 10 million citizens.

What matters is that people themselves are allowed to determine how large the administrative units are in which they want to live and what form of government they have. It need not be democracy. Liechtenstein (160 km2), Monaco (2 km2), Dubai, Hong Kong (1100 km2) and Singapore (710 km2) are not parliamentary democracies. But they are successful. These countries show that often 'small is beautiful'.

One might think that the right to secede and self-government leads to conflicts. But that does not follow. Consider how the free market works. Everyone has the right to start a business. Still, the majority of people are employed by companies. Such cooperation brings benefits to all parties. That applies to countries too. People may choose to be independent, but most will find it in their interest to join a society. And the various societies will also find it in their interest to cooperate. Sure, economies of scale can reduce costs, but at what scale this will happen can only be determined if people are free to choose.

Secession does not necessarily have to lead to full administrative autonomy right away. Any form of decentralization in which certain responsibilities are transferred from central to local government could be called political secession. This could be an attractive (transitional) form between complete secession and the current situation.

How this could work can be seen in the example of the so-called Special Economic Zones like Shenzhen that the Chinese government created in the 1980s and 1990s. These regions had little regulation, allowed some foreign investment and paved the way for the rest of China to become more free. Dubai has also set up such free-trade zones where few trade and labor regulations exist. Such Economic Free Zones could be a model for Political Free Zones where people could experiment with different forms of governance.

The contractual society

People often think that if the state does not provide something (e.g. pay for the opera, or care for the elderly), it won't happen. But that is the mentality of people in the former Soviet Union who said: where would we be if the state no longer takes care of us? When the American economist Milton Friedman visited communist China he was asked by officials who the US Secretary of Natural Resources was. When he told them there was no such person, they stared at him in disbelief. They couldn't imagine that production and distribution of raw materials was possible without government control.

In the past, people could not imagine what life would be like without a king. The king was expected to provide for his subjects. We now look at the State and democracy in the same way. Today people find it difficult to imagine that citizens – before the advent of democracy – accepted the authority of the king. But strangely they do accept the authority of the majority without a murmur.

> *Today people find it difficult to imagine that citizens – before the advent of democracy – accepted the authority of the king. But strangely they do accept the authority of the majority without a murmur.*

Yet we see self-organization without coercion and control from above happening around us every day. Often contrary to expectation. No one thought that something as anarchistic as Wikipedia, the Internet encyclopedia, could be successful without central control. But it works. The whole Internet is a collection of numerous separate organizations, individuals and technologies that work together without central management. At the start of the worldwide web many could not believe that the Internet had no owner, that it was based on individual voluntary arrangements between thousands of organizations (internet service providers, companies, institutions), each of them controlling a small fraction of the network.

In fact, our ideal and free society would be similar to the model the Internet is based on. With the internet, only a few simple rules apply; the rest is open for everyone to participate in as they see fit. The main rule is to communicate via the internet protocol TCP/IP. On this basis, millions of companies, organizations and individuals are free to do their own thing – set up their own domains, offer their services and communicate in the way they want. People can also start new protocols on top of TCP/IP and find out if others want to follow their lead. They can start new services and see if they can find customers. This diversity, freedom and self-organization on the Internet has proven to work amazingly well.

Similarly, in a free society, the main rule is not to commit fraud, violence and theft. As long as people keep to this rule, they can offer any services, including what are now viewed as

> *A free society would be similar to the model the Internet is based on. With the internet, only a few simple rules apply; the rest is open for everyone to participate in as they see fit.*

'public' services. They can also set up their own communities as they see fit – monarchist, communist, conservative, religious or even authoritarian, as long as their 'customers' join voluntarily and as long as they leave other organizations alone. And those communities can be as small as ten people or as big as a million (note that a private company like Walmart has two million employees).

When you have many different administrative units, people can always move if they don't like things and the rulers are well aware of this. Their residents are not merely citizens who are occasionally allowed to vote but customers they have to serve well in order to retain them. The same happens in the market. If customers don't like what the baker has to offer they don't organize protests in order to influence the owner, they just go to another bakery.

Small societies are more likely to be based on clear agreements than on influence through the ballot box. In the US and other democratic countries, no citizen has a contract with the government specifying their mutual obligations, e.g. what the government will provide and at what cost. Think of issues such as pensions, health care, education, subsidies, labor laws, and so on. Citizens have a vague and undefined obligation to pay taxes and to abide by laws, whereas the government has an undefined obligation to provide services. And the government can change the rules at any time, regardless of any election results. This creates considerable legal uncertainty. You may have paid pension contributions for years with the expectation that upon retirement you will receive certain benefits. Yet the government can change the amount of those benefits with the stroke of a pen. Or you rent out a room thinking that you can cancel the lease at a certain time, when the government suddenly decides that different conditions will apply to the required length of leases.

A decent society should be based on contracts where rights are respected and all parties know where they stand. Where rules can't be changed during the game by the rulers. And those contracts don't necessarily have to be the same for everyone. Just like with employees of a company, different citizens could have different contracts, depending on the area where they live or work.

> *In the US and other democratic countries, no citizen has a contract with the government specifying their mutual obligations, e.g. what the government will provide and at what cost.*

The road to freedom

If technological progress is an indication of future developments, then the prospects of decentralization are bright. A technological invention such as the car liberated people in their mobility. The invention of the pill gave people more sexual freedom and women more control over their lives. The arrival of the Internet put an end to the ruling elite's stranglehold on the media. Now everyone can publish news, send his ideas into the world or start selling products on the Internet.

In fact, technology is the truly democratizing force, more so than the democratic system itself. Whereas democracy gives power to the majority to rule over the minority, technology tends to offer individuals power over their own lives. Democracy takes power away from individuals, technology empowers them. It's a decentralizing force that can render the middleman, the government, superfluous in matters like communication, finance, education, the media, and trade. And since the free market makes technology ever cheaper, it gives even the poorest people some control over their own destiny. Even in Africa nowadays millions of people get new opportunities, not because of development aid, but thanks to computers and mobile phones that keep getting cheaper.

Thus, mankind experienced a great deal of progress during the last century, not because of democracy, but because of technology and private enterprise. Appliances such as the iPhone, the Walkman, and the PC have brought advanced technological capabilities within reach of the individual and contributed towards his emancipation. Through services such as Facebook, individuals are able to choose what social contexts they want to belong to, even across national boundaries, and without government interference. In addition, the development of English as a world language and the possibility to travel cheaply have made the word 'smaller' and have made it easier to move to other countries.

All this implies that competition with regard to governance might work very well. Already people increasingly choose where they want

> *In fact, technology is the truly democratizing force, more so than the democratic system itself.*

to work or live and under what sort of governance. Millions of people live or work abroad. A world with many small governmental units, each with their own characteristics, would be in line with these developments. These small units can choose to cooperate on certain issues if that is to their advantage, e.g. in energy, immigration, and transportation. They could also cooperate on defense, which could be important if a Big State were to arise that wanted to crush the smaller societies. Economically successful and innovative societies would most likely find smart ways to defend themselves against this kind of aggression.

New technology even allows for the creation of entirely new countries. The Seasteading organization co-founded by the aforementioned Patri Friedman, is trying to build artificial islands in international waters. These islands can provide alternatives to existing forms of government.

In order to achieve decentralization, our current political system is in need of radical changes, but they are not as difficult to realize as one might think. Large government organizations can be dismantled. Ministries of education, health, social affairs, economic affairs, agriculture, foreign affairs, development aid and finance can be discarded. A society only needs basic public services to ensure law and order and to deal with environmental issues.

The welfare state can be converted into a private insurance system. This will allow citizens freedom and security. They will be able to take out insurance individually or collectively through trade unions or the companies they work for. The state insurance as we know it is constantly subject to arbitrary changes by the government. The security the State promises is a false one and is subject to political whim. This must stop. Care for the poor and the needy can be provided locally.

Government control of our financial system should be abolished so that governments can no longer erode the value of our money, and cause booms and busts. In this way a fair international financial market would be created, no longer manipulated by powerful governments and government-related financial institutions.

In short, the large democratic nation-state has to make way for smaller political units in which citizens themselves choose how they want to shape their society. Wherever possible matters should be decided upon locally at the lowest possible administrative level.

If that means the end of the European Union, so much the better. Politicians in Europe love to paint doomsday scenarios about what would happen if the European Union were to fall apart. But countries such as Norway and Switzerland have never been members of the EU and do very well on their own.

It is sometimes argued that the EU ensures free trade among European countries. If that was the only thing it did, it would be fine, but it does a lot more. The 'internal market' created by Brussels has nothing to do with economic freedom. On the contrary. The EU virtually oozes laws and regulations that restrict economic freedom. It is a Super State under construction which will destroy the freedom of citizens and businesses alike. The EU represents the opposite of decentralization - it is the epitome of centralization, an unworkable bureaucratic juggernaut, where individual freedom is even more threatened than in a national democracy. The sooner it is abolished the better.

A bright future

In many ways, the future looks bright. Mankind has accumulated tremendous knowledge and a huge production capacity – more than enough to create prosperity for everyone in the world.

In addition, after the collapse of the bloody communist and fascist regimes of the 20th century, such as in the Soviet Union, China and other countries, there is a worldwide trend towards more freedom. Large groups of people have gained more personal and economic freedom, leading to greater prosperity and well-being. Others are rising up against dictatorships and demanding more freedom. There is no reason why this trend shouldn't continue.

It may be hard to imagine that life is possible without the Democratic Nation-State, but similar radical changes have taken place in the past. As Linda and Morris Tannehill wrote in their classic libertarian, anti-democratic book The Market For Liberty (1970): "Imagine a feudal serf, legally bound to the land he was born on and to the social position he was born into, toiling from dawn to dusk with primitive tools for a bare subsistence which he must share with the lord of his manor, his mental processes enmeshed with fears and superstitions. Imagine trying to tell this serf about the social structure of Twentieth Century America. You would probably have a hard time convincing him that such a social structure could exist at all, because he would view everything you described from the context of his own knowledge of society. He would inform you, no doubt with a trace of smug superiority, that unless each individual born into the community had a specific and permanently fixed social place, society would speedily deteriorate into chaos. In a similar way, telling a Twentieth Century man that government is evil and, therefore, unnecessary, and that we would have a far better society if we had no government at all, is likely to elicit polite skepticism … especially if the man is not used to thinking independently. It is always difficult to picture the workings of society different from our own, and particularly a more advanced society. This is because we are so used to our own social structure that we tend to automatically consider each facet of the more advanced society in the context of our own, thus distorting the picture into meaninglessness."

We believe that the nation-state and the democracy that goes with it are phenomena of the 20th century, not of the 21st century. The road to autonomy and empowerment will continue but it will not lead through large democracies. It will lead through decentralization and the organization of people into smaller administrative units, designed by the people themselves.

Some might argue that most people are not capable of being free. That they don't have the responsibility or desire to live independent lives. That they should be governed for their own good. But this is the same argument that was used against the abolition of slavery or the emancipation of women. Slavery should not be abolished, it was argued, because blacks would be unable to take care of themselves – and anyway, most would not even want to be free. Women should not have equal rights, it was said, because they are incapable of earning their own living and dealing with the demands of an independent life. But reality proved otherwise. It will be the same when the democratic Nanny state is abolished. People will turn out be surprisingly self-reliant when they get the chance. Of course they will not decide to live individualistically, but will self-organize in groups of their own choosing, in companies, clubs, trade unions, associations, special interest groups, communities and families.

Released from the stultifying control of bureaucracy and democratic majority-rule, they will change the world in ways that we cannot foresee now. As Linda and Morris Tannehill put it: "Many undesirable conditions which people take for granted today would be different in a society totally free of government. Most of these differences would spring from a market liberated from the dead hand of government control — both fascist and socialist — and thus able to produce a healthy economy and a vastly higher standard of living for everyone."

It's time for people to wake up to the fact that democracy does not lead to liberty or autonomy. It does not solve conflicts and it does not unleash productive and creative forces. Quite the opposite. Democracy creates antagonism and restrictions. The centralist and compulsive aspects of democracy result in organized chaos, whereas individual freedom and the dynamics of the unorganized market bring spontaneous order and prosperity.

> *For themselves, people prefer freedom to coercion. They prefer having a direct choice on the free market to merely indicating their preference in the voting booth.*

For themselves, people prefer freedom to coercion. They prefer having a direct choice on the free market to merely indicating their preference in the voting booth. Is there anyone who would prefer the government to choose their car for them rather than they could choose their own car?

It is high time that people realize that the freedom they wish for themselves, must also be given to others. That their freedom cannot last if others do not enjoy the same freedom. That in the end they themselves will become the victims of the coercion that they - democratically - exert over others. They will fall into a trap of their own making.

A movement towards less democracy and more freedom might seem frightening to some. We have all grown up in national-democratic nation states and have been endlessly subjected to social democratic ideas. We have been taught that our society is 'the best of all possible worlds.'

However, the reality is less appealing. It's time to face up to that reality. Government is not a benevolent Santa Claus. It is a selfish, interfering monster that will never be satisfied and will eventually suffocate the independence and autonomy of its subjects. And this monster is sustained by democracy: By the idea that the life of every human being may be controlled by the majority.

It is time to abandon the idea that the People - and thus the State - have the right to rule. That we will be better off if governments determine how we live and spend our money rather than that we do this ourselves. That the democratic one-size-fits-all ideology will bring harmony and prosperity. That we benefit from democratic coercion.

It's time to free ourselves from the tyranny of the majority. We have nothing to lose but the chains that bind us to each other.

Postscript

Libertarianism and democracy

Our critique of democracy was written from a libertarian perspective. Libertarianism is a political philosophy based on self-ownership, i.e. the right of every individual to his own body and life and thus the fruits of his labor. The alternative to self government is that some people rule over the lives and labor of others (or − but this is highly unrealistic − that everyone rules over everyone). According to libertarianism such a situation is unjust. Libertarianism is based on the principle that individuals have no obligation to sacrifice themselves to the collective, as is the case under socialism, fascism and democracy.

For libertarians individual liberty (self-ownership) does not mean the 'right' to work, education, health care, housing or some other good, since such 'rights' imply the duty of others to provide those benefits. If a person is forced to sacrifice himself for others, that's not liberty, but slavery. Liberty means that everybody has the right to do what they want with their lives and property, as long as they do not interfere with the lives and property of others. In short, libertarians are against the initiation of physical force.

The primary purpose of the libertarian system of justice is to protect the individual against all forms of force. Libertarians are in favor of all liberties which follow from the principle of self-government. For example, we are for freedom of religion, freedom of euthanasia, legalization of drugs, free speech, and so on. We are also for the right of people to associate, cooperate and trade freely, i.e. for a free market.

We believe individuals and groups have the right to make their own rules concerning the use of their property. Just as everybody is allowed to decide whom he invites into his home, the owner of a bar should be allowed to decide if smoking is permitted in his bar and an employer should be allowed to decide on a dress code within his company. Anyone is free not to visit a bar, or not to work for a company, if they don't like the rules.

For this reason, libertarianism is against anti-discrimination laws. Such laws are incompatible with the principle of free association. Government decrees: *Thou shalt associate! Whether you like it or not.* In contrast, libertarianism is based on freedom of choice; all relations and transactions should be voluntary.

Discrimination means: To treat differently. Of course it's ridiculous not to want to associate with gays, Jews, Germans or whomever, but the principle of liberty means nobody has to justify his choices, no matter how ridiculous. You don't need a good reason not to do something. Libertarianism defends the right of people to do things, or not to do things, which may be disagreeable to others. Just as free speech means that people have the right to express an opinion that others disagree with. People's sole obligation is to refrain from initiating force toward others.

Anti-discrimination laws are, in fact, themselves a form of force, since they force people to associate with others against their will. Should we force old ladies to enter dark alleys where violent youths hang out? Should we force people to go on dates with people they find unattractive? Of course not. But then by what right does government force employers to employ people they don't want to employ? And by what right does government force night club owners to accept customers they don't want? As libertarians we believe that such forms are not only wrong, but also counterproductive. They lead to hatred and conflicts rather than tolerance and harmony.

Libertarianism is neither 'leftist' nor 'rightist', neither progressive nor conservative. Progressives favor government interference in the economy but are willing (sometimes) to allow a reasonable degree of personal freedom. Conservatives favor government interference with personal choices but are willing (sometimes) to allow a reasonable degree of economic freedom. But both have in common that they consider the individual a subject of the State, of the collective. Libertarianism is the only political philosophy which says that the collective does *not* have the right to rule the individual. Libertarianism is the only political philosophy which is against *the initiation of force* in principle, i.e. against all use of force except in self-defense. Based on this principle libertarianism is also against colonialism, imperialism and foreign interventions.

Libertarianism is not a new-fangled philosophy; it is based on an age-old tradition. The ideas of the great liberal 17th and 18th Century thinkers were very close to the libertarian ideal. Today we denote their philosophy as 'classical liberal' to distinguish it from the current 'liberalism', which is really a variant of social democracy rather than a philosophy of liberty. In the 19th Century libertarianism was defended both by a number of 'anarcho-capitalists' and a group of classical liberal economists, mainly from Austria. A current academic center of libertarianism in the US is the Mises Institute, named after the great Austrian free market economist Ludwig von Mises. In 1974 Friedrich Hayek, a student of Mises, received the Nobel prize in economics. The most famous 20th century libertarian thinker was another student of Mises, the American economist and all-round intellectual Murray Rothbard. His book *For a New Liberty* is probably still the best introduction to libertarianism available.

However, Mises and Rothbard never produced a rigorous analysis of the phenomenon of democracy. The first libertarian thinker to do so is the German economist Hans-Hermann Hoppe, who lives and works in the US. His book *Democracy – The God that Failed* (2001) is for the time being the standard libertarian work in this area.

In recent years, partly thanks to Hoppe's work, the idea of democracy has been getting more attention from libertarian writers, but most of their criticisms are to be found only in articles published in various magazines and on libertarian websites such as Mises.org. As far as we know, no full-fledged popular libertarian critique of democracy has ever been published. We hope to have filled this gap with this book.

For more information about this book, see our website *www.beyonddemocracy.net*. In the Netherlands more information about libertarianism can be found on the Dutch-language website of Frank Karsten, *www.meervrijheid.nl.*

Some quotes on democracy

"*Democracy is two wolves and a lamb voting on what to have for lunch. Liberty is a well-armed lamb contesting the vote.*"
Benjamin Franklin, statesman, scientist, philosopher, and one of the founding fathers of the United States

"*Democracy never lasts long. It soon wastes, exhausts, and murders itself. There is never a democracy that did not commit suicide.*"
John Adams, second president of the United States

"*Democracy is nothing more than mob rule, where 51% of the people may take away the rights of the other 49%.*"
Thomas Jefferson, third president of the United States

"*We believe socialism and democracy are one and indivisible.*"
Socialist Party U.S.A.

"*Every election is sort of an advance auction sale of stolen goods.*"
H.L. Mencken (1880 - 1956), American journalist and essayist

"*How can we continue to ensure progress if we increasingly adopt a lifestyle in which nobody is willing to take responsibility for themselves and everyone is looking for safety in collectivism? If this mania continues, we will decline into a social system in which everyone has their hands in the pockets of others.*"
Ludwig Erhard, former German Chancellor and architect of the postwar German economic miracle

"*Unlimited democracy is, just like oligarchy, a tyranny spread over a large number of people.*"
Aristotle

"*Government is the great fiction through which everybody endeavors to live at the expense of everybody else.*"

Frédéric Bastiat (1801 - 1850), French classical liberal theorist and political economist

"When the people find that they can vote themselves money, that will herald the end of the republic."
Benjamin Franklin, statesman, scientist, philosopher, and one of the founding fathers of the United States

"Those who are asking for more government interference are asking ultimately for more compulsion and less freedom."
Ludwig von Mises, Austrian economist and great free market defender

"No man's life, liberty, or property are safe while the legislature is in session."
Mark Twain (1835 – 1910), American author

"Democracy is the will of the people. Every morning I am surprised to read in the newspaper what I want."
Wim Kan, Dutch comedian

This space for notes

This space for notes

This space for notes

This space for notes

Made in the USA
Lexington, KY
22 June 2012